THE TRUTH UNVEILED: MASTERING THE ART OF READING PEOPLE

LEGAL DISCLAIMER AND COPYRIGHT NOTICE

TABLE OF CONTENTS

SAM TIWANA

DEDICATION

This book is dedicated to the countless individuals who have unknowingly contributed to its creation—those whose subtle gestures, fleeting expressions, and nuanced postures have provided invaluable lessons in the intricate dance of human communication. It is a tribute to the inherent human capacity for connection, even in the unspoken moments. To those who have shown the power of empathy and understanding, even amidst misunderstanding, this work is gratefully offered. It is also dedicated to the persistent seekers of truth, those who strive to unravel the mysteries of human interaction, and who embrace the challenge of deeper understanding. Their curiosity and dedication inspire us all to look beyond the surface and to truly see. Finally, this book is dedicated to the silent language itself; the rich tapestry of nonverbal cues that reveal the depths of human experience.

May this work serve as a guide to understanding and appreciating its complexity and power. May it illuminate the path towards more authentic, fulfilling connections, and a deeper understanding of ourselves and each other.

PREFACE

We live in a world of constant communication, yet so much of what we convey is unspoken. The subtle shifts in posture, the fleeting expressions that cross our faces, the unconscious gestures of our hands – these are the silent languages that speak volumes about our thoughts, feelings, and intentions. "The Truth Unveiled: Mastering the Art of Reading People" offers a practical exploration into this fascinating world of nonverbal communication. This book is not about manipulation or judgment; rather, it's about empowerment and understanding. It provides a framework for developing keen observational skills and enhancing your ability to interpret the complex signals that human beings exchange constantly. Whether you're a professional seeking to improve your negotiation skills, a parent navigating family dynamics, or simply someone interested in deepening human connections, the insights presented within these pages will provide invaluable tools for enhanced communication and more fulfilling relationships. We have strived to make this complex subject accessible and engaging through clear explanations, practical exercises, and compelling real-world examples. By the end of this book, you will be better equipped to decipher the subtle cues that others emit, fostering empathy, enhancing your communication prowess, and leading to more authentic and meaningful interactions. Prepare to uncover the secrets hidden beneath the surface, and embark on a journey of insightful self-discovery. The truth, as you'll discover, is often found not in what is said, but in what is shown.

INTRODUCTION

Human beings are inherently social creatures, constantly communicating and seeking connection. Yet, our communication is far more nuanced than the simple exchange of words. A significant portion of our daily
interactions is governed by nonverbal cues – the unspoken language of body language, facial expressions, and subtle gestures. "The Truth Unveiled: Mastering the Art of Reading People" delves into this often-overlooked realm of human interaction, equipping you with the knowledge and skills to interpret these vital nonverbal signals. This book is not about mind-reading or deception detection, although those elements are certainly touched upon. Its primary focus is on fostering a deeper understanding of human communication in all its complexity. Through the exploration of microexpressions, body posture, hand gestures, and eye movements, you will gain the tools to enhance your observational skills and cultivate a more perceptive understanding of yourself and others. This increased awareness will improve your ability to build stronger, more authentic relationships, navigate challenging social situations with greater confidence, and ultimately, lead a more fulfilling life. The journey to mastering the art of reading people begins with self-awareness and a commitment to

mindful observation. Throughout this book, we will guide you through practical exercises, real-world examples, and detailed explanations to help you integrate this knowledge into your daily interactions. We will explore the cultural nuances of nonverbal communication, emphasizing the importance of context and avoiding generalizations. Furthermore, we will stress the ethical considerations surrounding interpretation of nonverbal cues, encouraging responsible and respectful engagement with this powerful form of communication. Prepare to embark on an exciting journey of discovery – the truth, as you will soon find, is often hidden in plain sight.

UNDERSTANDING THE POWER OF NONVERBAL CUES

We often believe that words hold the key to understanding others, but the truth lies far beyond the spoken word. The realm of nonverbal communication, a silent language woven into our every movement, gesture, and expression, holds a power that often surpasses the clarity of spoken language.

This silent language, a complex tapestry of subtle cues, speaks volumes about a person's true thoughts, feelings, and intentions. Mastering the art of interpreting these nonverbal cues is not merely a skill; it's a key to unlocking deeper understanding in your personal and professional life.

Consider a simple scenario: a friend tells you, "I'm fine," but their shoulders are slumped, their voice is flat, and their gaze is averted. Do their words truly reflect their internal state?

Likely not. The incongruence between their verbal and nonverbal signals hints at something more – perhaps sadness, frustration, or even anger. This subtle disconnect is a prime example of the power of nonverbal cues; they often betray hidden emotions and intentions far more eloquently than words alone.

The human brain is remarkably adept at processing nonverbal information. Studies have shown that a significant portion of our communication, up to 93% according to some researchers, is nonverbal. This includes a wide range of cues: facial expressions, eye movements, posture, gestures, tone of voice, proximity, and even the subtle shifts in our breathing patterns. Each of these cues contributes to a complex communication narrative, often unconsciously conveying information that we may not even be aware of ourselves. Understanding nonverbal communication isn't about becoming a mind reader; it's about becoming a more perceptive observer. It's about learning to notice these subtle signals, understand their potential meanings, and interpret them within the broader context of the interaction. This requires a shift in perspective, a move away from focusing solely on words and towards recognizing the wealth of information conveyed through the body's unspoken language.

The impact of nonverbal communication extends far beyond simple social interactions. In professional settings, the ability to read nonverbal cues can be crucial for success.
Negotiators who can detect subtle signs of discomfort or deception during a deal have a significant advantage.
Salespeople who understand how to create rapport through appropriate body language can close deals more effectively. HR professionals skilled in

reading nonverbal cues can make more informed hiring decisions. Law enforcement officers who are adept at observing nonverbal indicators can gain valuable insights during interrogations. The list extends to countless professions where accurate interpretation of nonverbal communication can dramatically improve outcomes.

Conversely, a lack of understanding in nonverbal communication can lead to misinterpretations, misunderstandings, and even damaged relationships. Failing to recognize the unspoken signals can lead to missed
opportunities, misjudgments, and potentially, the erosion of trust. In personal relationships, the ability to decipher nonverbal cues can foster stronger connections, improve conflict resolution, and build more authentic bonds. By understanding how your own body language impacts others and how to interpret others' nonverbal signals, you can cultivate more empathetic and meaningful interactions.

The concept of congruency and incongruency is central to understanding the power of nonverbal cues. Congruency refers to the alignment between verbal and nonverbal
messages. When words and body language consistently communicate the same message, it reinforces the clarity and sincerity of the communication. Incongruency, on the other hand, arises when the verbal and nonverbal messages contradict each other. This is where the true art of interpretation comes into play. As previously illustrated, if someone says they are "fine" but their body language

portrays something different, the nonverbal signals often hold more weight. This is because our subconscious often leaks true emotions through our body language, regardless of what we consciously choose to say.

Consider the impact of posture. An open posture, with arms uncrossed and legs relaxed, typically indicates openness, confidence, and receptiveness. A closed posture, with arms crossed or legs tightly together, suggests defensiveness, anxiety, or a reluctance to engage. A slight head tilt can signal interest or attentiveness; a direct stare might indicate dominance or aggression, while averted gaze can suggest discomfort, shyness, or deception. These are just a few examples of how subtle changes in body position can significantly alter the interpretation of a message. Even seemingly minor variations in tone of voice can drastically change the meaning. A sharp, harsh tone may convey anger, while a soft, gentle tone can express warmth and understanding. Similarly, subtle changes in pace or rhythm of speech can add layers of meaning to a verbal message.

Another crucial aspect to grasp is the importance of context. Nonverbal cues should never be interpreted in isolation. The same gesture, expression, or posture can hold vastly different meanings depending on the situation, the individuals involved, and the cultural context. A firm handshake might signify confidence in one culture but aggression in another. A prolonged eye contact may indicate interest and attraction in some contexts but challenge and hostility in others. Always consider the surrounding circumstances before jumping to conclusions.

This understanding requires careful and mindful observation. Practicing attentiveness to details, honing your observational skills, and immersing yourself in understanding the nuances of nonverbal communication are vital steps. Observational skills are essential, and they can be developed with diligent practice, focusing on paying attention to the subtle signals people send unconsciously.

Moreover, understanding the concept of baseline behavior is critical for accurate interpretation. A baseline refers to an individual's typical or normal behavior in a particular context. By observing a person's normal nonverbal patterns, you can establish a baseline against which to measure deviations. Changes from that baseline often provide
valuable insights into their emotional state or intentions. A person who usually maintains a relaxed posture and suddenly becomes rigid may be experiencing anxiety or discomfort. Someone who typically makes frequent eye contact and then avoids eye contact may be attempting to conceal something.

In conclusion, the power of nonverbal cues lies in their ability to reveal what words often conceal. By becoming attuned to these subtle signals, we can significantly enhance our ability to understand others, build stronger relationships, navigate social situations with greater confidence, and achieve greater success in our professional lives. This first chapter lays the groundwork, offering the fundamental understanding you need to embark on the journey to mastering the art of reading people. The subsequent chapters will delve into more specific techniques, providing practical exercises and real-world examples to solidify your understanding and help you develop your observational skills. Remember, this is not about manipulation; it's about developing deeper empathy and building more authentic connections with the people around you.

THE MICROEXPRESSION MASTERCLASS

The foundation we've laid – understanding the pervasive influence of nonverbal communication – now leads us to a crucial aspect: decoding facial expressions. While spoken words may attempt to mask emotions, the face, often unwittingly, reveals the truth. This isn't about simply noting a smile or a frown; it's about discerning the subtle shifts, the fleeting expressions that betray the true emotional landscape beneath the surface. These fleeting expressions, known as microexpressions, are the key to unlocking a deeper
understanding of human behavior.

Microexpressions are involuntary, rapid facial muscle movements that reveal genuine emotions, often contradicting the consciously displayed expressions. They are incredibly brief, lasting only a fraction of a second – typically between 1/25th and 1/5th of a second – making them difficult to detect without focused attention and practice. Unlike
macroexpressions – the more obvious and prolonged facial expressions we consciously

control – microexpressions are almost impossible to suppress completely. This involuntary nature makes them a powerful tool for detecting genuine emotion, even when someone is actively trying to conceal their feelings.

Imagine a scenario: a colleague tells you they're delighted with a new project assignment, yet a quick flash of a furrowed brow and slightly tightened lips – lasting mere milliseconds – crosses their face. This brief microexpression, if detected, suggests a potential underlying feeling of apprehension or dislike, contradicting the verbal expression of delight. Understanding this discrepancy offers invaluable insight into their true feelings about the project and allows you to approach the situation with greater sensitivity and understanding. This is the power of recognizing microexpressions.

The primary emotions reflected in microexpressions are generally considered to be universal: happiness, sadness, anger, fear, surprise, and disgust. These basic emotions form the building blocks of our more complex emotional experiences. Recognizing these basic microexpressions is the first crucial step in mastering the art of reading people.

Let's delve deeper into each of these basic emotions and their corresponding microexpressions:

Happiness:
A genuine smile, unlike a forced one, involves the contraction of muscles around the eyes (the "crow's feet"), creating wrinkles at the corners. A false smile typically only involves the muscles of

the mouth. Observe for a brief, fleeting lifting of the cheeks and a crinkling around the eyes. The expression may be incredibly brief, almost imperceptible, but the subtle contraction of the muscles around the eyes is the key differentiator.

Sadness:
Sadness often manifests as a downturning of the mouth, but microexpressions associated with sadness might involve a slight drooping of the eyelids, a slight tightening of the eyebrows, and a subtle lowering of the corners of the mouth. The entire expression may be fleeting, almost like a shadow passing across the face, but the subtle downward pull of the mouth and eyes is the telltale sign. Look for a very brief, almost invisible, tightening of the lips, which might occur before the individual attempts to mask their sadness with a forced smile.

Anger:
A microexpression of anger might involve a tightening of the lips, a furrowing of the eyebrows, and possibly a slight widening of the eyes. The tightening of the lips can be quite subtle, almost undetectable unless you are specifically looking for it. It's the sudden, brief intensity of the furrow in the brow that distinguishes an angry microexpression from a mere pensive expression. A quick clenching of the jaw might also be a clue.

Fear:
Fear often triggers a widening of the eyes, a slight raising of the eyebrows, and possibly a slight opening of the mouth. The eyebrows may

be slightly raised and pulled inwards, and the eyes may be slightly widened in a brief, barely perceptible display of fear. The expression may disappear almost as quickly as it appears, but the widened eyes and raised eyebrows are the key elements. The lips might also slightly pull back from the teeth in a fleeting expression.

Surprise:

Surprise is generally characterized by a widening of the eyes, a raising of the eyebrows, and sometimes a slight opening of the mouth. The eyebrows arch quickly, almost instantaneously, and the eyes open wide. This is often accompanied by a slight backward pull of the head. Unlike fear, however, the overall impression is one of openness and widened eyes rather than a sense of apprehension. It's the speed and abruptness of the widening of the eyes that is a key indicator.

Disgust:

Disgust is often expressed through a wrinkling of the nose, a raising of the upper lip, and sometimes a slight turning away of the head. The nose might wrinkle slightly, the upper lip may lift, and the entire facial expression will convey a sense of rejection and aversion. The speed and subtlety of the expression are key to identifying it as a microexpression. The combination of the nose wrinkle and the lip raise is what distinguishes this from other expressions.

Practical Exercises:

To improve your ability to detect microexpressions, consistent practice is essential. Here are a few exercises you can perform:

1.

Watch videos:

Search online for videos specifically designed for microexpression training. Many videos feature individuals displaying brief emotional expressions, allowing you to practice identifying them. Repeat viewing is crucial.

Slowing down the footage can significantly improve your ability to detect the subtle changes.

2.

Analyze movies and TV shows:

Pay close attention to the actors' faces. Look for those brief, fleeting changes in expression that might reveal their character's true emotions, even if their dialogue suggests otherwise. Focus on the nuances of their facial expressions.

3.

Observe people in real life:

Practice observing people in everyday situations. Pay attention to their facial expressions, and try to identify microexpressions. Start by observing friends and family members in comfortable settings, then gradually move towards observing strangers. Remember, ethical considerations are paramount. Never invade anyone's privacy.

4.

Use mirror practice:

Practice making different facial expressions yourself. Start with the basic emotions, then try to produce the microexpressions. This will help you understand the subtle muscular movements involved. This helps you build an internal map of these expressions.

5.
Use photographs:
Find photographs of individuals displaying various emotions. Focus on the subtle details of their facial expressions, paying particular attention to the muscles around the eyes, the mouth, and the eyebrows.

6.
Work with a partner:
Have a partner intentionally display brief emotional expressions while you try to identify them. Then switch roles. This form of feedback is invaluable in improving your observation skills.

Mastering the art of detecting microexpressions isn't about becoming a mind reader; it's about developing a heightened awareness of nonverbal cues, enhancing your ability to perceive and understand others' emotions more accurately.
The more you practice, the better you will become at recognizing these fleeting indicators of genuine emotion, allowing you to build stronger relationships, navigate challenging situations with greater confidence, and make more informed judgments about people's true intentions.
Remember, this skill takes time and dedication, but the rewards are well worth the effort. The ability to interpret microexpressions is a powerful tool that will enrich your life significantly. It's a journey of continuous learning and refinement, constantly sharpening your observational skills and empowering you to navigate the complex

world of human interaction with greater insight and understanding.

GAZE BLINKS AND PUPIL DILATION

Building upon our understanding of microexpressions and their revealing nature, we now delve into another crucial aspect of nonverbal communication: the language of the eyes. While the face as a whole offers a wealth of information, the eyes, often called "the windows to the soul," provide a uniquely intimate glimpse into a person's inner world. Their movements, subtle shifts, and even the slightest changes in dilation speak volumes, often revealing information that words cannot, or perhaps will not, convey.

The power of eye contact is undeniable. A prolonged gaze can signal intense interest, attraction, or even dominance, depending on the context. Conversely, a lack of eye contact can indicate shyness, discomfort, deception, or a desire to avoid interaction. However, it's crucial to avoid simplistic interpretations. Cultural norms significantly influence eye contact patterns. In some cultures, prolonged eye contact is considered respectful and engaging, while in others it can be seen as aggressive or challenging. A person from a culture that avoids prolonged eye contact might be misinterpreted as being shifty or untrustworthy by someone from a culture where direct eye contact is the norm. This underscores the importance of considering the cultural context when interpreting eye behavior.

Beyond the duration of eye contact, the direction of the gaze also offers valuable insights. When someone is recalling a memory, their gaze often drifts upward and to the left or right, depending on their dominant hemisphere. This is because accessing memory involves different parts of the brain, and the eye movements often reflect this internal cognitive process. Similarly, when someone is constructing a lie, their gaze might dart around, suggesting an internal struggle to maintain coherence in their fabricated narrative. However, it's essential to acknowledge that these are general tendencies and not absolute rules. Individual variations exist, and other factors can influence eye movements. The key is to observe the patterns and inconsistencies rather than relying on isolated instances. Blink rate is another subtle yet telling aspect of eye behavior.

A significantly increased blink rate can indicate stress, anxiety, or deception. When a person is under pressure or attempting to conceal something, their blinking might become more frequent or more rapid, betraying their internal state. Conversely, a decreased blink rate might suggest intense focus or concentration. However, it is crucial to note that individual baseline blink rates vary considerably. Some people naturally blink more frequently than others.

Therefore, the focus should be on noticeable changes in a person's typical blinking pattern, rather than making generalizations based on an arbitrary number of blinks per minute.

Pupil dilation, a less consciously controlled aspect of eye behavior, offers a fascinating glimpse into a person's emotional and cognitive state. Pupils dilate in response to stimuli that the brain finds interesting or emotionally arousing. This dilation can occur whether the stimulus is positive (like seeing something attractive) or negative (like experiencing fear or threat). Interestingly, studies have shown that pupil dilation can even be a subconscious indicator of attraction or interest, providing a subtle signal that may be overlooked even by the person experiencing it. However, environmental factors such as lighting conditions can influence pupil size, making it essential to consider the context. If the room is dimly lit, larger pupils might be simply a response to low light levels rather than a strong emotional reaction.

Let's consider practical applications of these observations.
Imagine you're in a business negotiation. Your counterpart avoids direct eye contact, blinks frequently, and their pupils are constricted. This combination might suggest
nervousness, discomfort, or even deception. Understanding this nonverbal communication could influence your approach, prompting you to probe deeper, build rapport, or adjust your negotiation strategy accordingly. Alternatively, if you're meeting someone for a date and they maintain consistent eye contact, their pupils dilate slightly when they look at you, and they display a relaxed blink rate, it's a good indication of genuine interest and positive attraction.
Recognizing these subtle cues can drastically

increase your social awareness and improve your interpersonal interactions.

To enhance your ability to interpret eye behavior, consistent practice is essential. Engage in observational exercises. Start by simply observing people in various settings – coffee shops, public transportation, social gatherings – paying close attention to their eye contact, blink rate, and pupil dilation. Note the contexts, considering factors such as the emotional tone of the interaction, the relationship between the individuals involved, and the cultural background of the persons being observed. Attempt to correlate their eye
behavior with other nonverbal cues and verbal content to gain a more holistic understanding.

For example, observe a group discussion. Pay attention not only to who is speaking, but also who maintains eye contact with the speaker, who avoids eye contact, and how their blink rate and pupil size changes throughout the conversation. Do certain individuals exhibit consistent patterns in their eye behavior? Do these patterns correlate with their participation level or their apparent emotional state? What can you infer about the dynamics of the group based on the subtle nuances of eye behavior? By
systematically observing and analyzing these patterns, you'll gradually sharpen your perception and develop a more intuitive understanding of the silent language of the eyes.

Remember, interpreting nonverbal communication is not about reaching definitive conclusions based solely on eye behavior. It is about integrating these observations with other nonverbal cues and considering the overall context to formulate a more accurate and nuanced interpretation. A single blink or a fleeting glance should not be taken in isolation. Rather, it's the pattern of behavior, the combination of cues, and the understanding of the context that allows for a richer and more accurate reading of a person's intentions and emotions. Treat this process as a continuous learning experience, refining your observational skills and deepening your comprehension of the multifaceted nature of human communication.

Furthermore, it's important to understand the limitations of observing eye behavior. It's not a foolproof method for detecting deception or determining someone's true feelings.
Certain medical conditions or medications can affect eye movements and pupil dilation, leading to misinterpretations.
Therefore, it's crucial to approach the observation of eye behavior with a healthy dose of skepticism and critical thinking, avoiding overly simplistic or reductive conclusions. Instead, focus on the overall pattern of nonverbal communication and consider all relevant information before making any judgments. The goal is not to "catch someone out" but to cultivate a more insightful and empathetic understanding of human behavior.

Consider the case of a witness in a legal setting. A nervous witness might exhibit rapid blinking and avoid eye contact.
However, this could be due to stress, fear, or the inherent pressure of the situation, not necessarily an indication of deception. Similarly, a calm and

confident witness might maintain steady eye contact and a normal blink rate, but this doesn't automatically mean they are telling the truth. The crucial aspect is to integrate the observation of their eye behavior with other nonverbal cues, such as their posture, hand gestures, and tone of voice, as well as the consistency of their verbal narrative. Only by considering the totality of the communication can we form a more informed and reliable interpretation.

The art of interpreting nonverbal communication, particularly the subtle nuances of eye behavior, is a skill that develops over time and through dedicated practice. It requires patience, observation, and a willingness to learn and adapt. By honing your observational abilities, integrating context, and adopting a thoughtful and analytical approach, you will significantly enhance your ability to understand and connect with people on a deeper level. This isn't about manipulating or controlling others, but about fostering better communication, building stronger relationships, and navigating social interactions with greater confidence and understanding. Remember, understanding the language of the eyes is just one piece of the puzzle in unlocking the secrets of human interaction, a journey that continues throughout our lives as we refine our observational skills and broaden our understanding of the complex world of nonverbal communication.

UNVEILING HIDDEN MEANINGS

Building upon our exploration of the eyes as windows to the soul, we now turn our attention to another rich source of nonverbal information: the hands and the body's posture.

These often-overlooked elements of communication can reveal a wealth of information, offering insights into a person's emotional state, level of confidence, and even their subconscious intentions. Understanding the language of hand gestures and posture is crucial in developing a more complete and nuanced understanding of human behavior.

Hand gestures, seemingly simple movements, are far more complex than they initially appear. They are not merely random twitches or nervous habits; rather, they form a significant part of our nonverbal vocabulary. We can categorize hand gestures into several key types, each carrying its unique communicative weight.

Illustrators are perhaps the most common type. These gestures accompany speech, visually reinforcing or emphasizing verbal messages. Think of someone describing the size of a fish they caught, using their hands to demonstrate its length. The gesture isn't replacing the words; it's enhancing them, creating a more vivid and engaging communication. Observe the frequency and intensity of illustrators. A person who uses many, large illustrators may be enthusiastic and expressive, while someone who uses few, small ones might be more reserved or less engaged in the conversation. The style and precision of these gestures can also provide clues to a person's personality and level of thoughtfulness. Precise, controlled illustrators might suggest a methodical nature, whereas more erratic and expansive movements could indicate impulsivity or heightened emotion.

Emblems are distinct from illustrators in that they can stand alone, conveying a specific meaning without the need for accompanying speech. The thumbs-up sign, for instance, universally signifies approval or agreement. Other emblems may be culturally specific; a gesture that means one thing in one culture may have a completely different or even offensive meaning in another. Therefore, it's essential to consider the cultural context when interpreting emblems. The use of emblems often suggests a degree of confidence and familiarity with the situation and the people involved.
An abundance of emblems could indicate someone comfortable in their environment and assertive in their communication, whereas a scarcity might point towards shyness, uncertainty, or perhaps a conscious effort to remain understated. Analyzing the context of emblem usage – who they are used with, where they are used, and the associated verbal cues – is vital for accurate interpretation.

Adaptors are gestures that serve to satisfy a physical or emotional need. These often manifest as unconscious self-touching behaviors, such as fidgeting, hair-twirling, or nail-biting. While seemingly inconsequential, adaptors can reveal a person's level of anxiety or discomfort. Increased fidgeting or self-touching may indicate nervousness, stress, or a desire to escape an uncomfortable situation. The location of the self-touching can also be insightful. For example, touching the face might suggest deception or a need to hide emotions, while playing with jewelry could indicate boredom or a lack of engagement. Observing changes in adaptors during a conversation can be particularly illuminating; an increase in such behaviors might signal a shift in emotional state or a response to a specific piece of information.

Manipulators are a subset of adaptors that involve manipulating objects or one's own body. Examples include repeatedly adjusting clothing, playing with a pen, or
constantly shifting one's weight. Similar to adaptors, manipulators often indicate nervousness or discomfort.

However, the specific object or body part manipulated can offer additional insights. For instance, consistently adjusting a tie might suggest a need for self-assurance, while repeatedly fiddling with a piece of jewelry could represent a deeper emotional preoccupation or even a subconscious attempt to ground themselves. The frequency and intensity of manipulative gestures, coupled with other nonverbal cues, can provide a clearer picture of the underlying emotional state.

Beyond hand gestures, body posture speaks volumes about a person's inner state and intentions. Open postures, characterized by relaxed limbs, an upright stance, and
uncrossed arms and legs, generally indicate confidence, openness, and receptiveness. A person maintaining an open posture is likely feeling comfortable and at ease in their environment. They are more likely to be approachable and willing to engage in interaction.

Conversely, closed postures – arms crossed, legs crossed, hunched shoulders, and a generally withdrawn stance – often signal insecurity, defensiveness, or a lack of comfort. This posture can indicate a person is feeling threatened, uncomfortable, or uninterested in the interaction. It can serve as a protective barrier, both physically and emotionally. The degree of closure can also be revealing; someone with slightly crossed arms might be merely feeling a little hesitant, whereas someone with tightly crossed arms and legs, along with other nonverbal signs of discomfort, might be experiencing considerable stress or anxiety.

The angle of the body also provides valuable information. Directly facing someone suggests engagement and interest, whereas angling away could suggest disinterest or a desire to escape the conversation. Leans also matter; leaning forward often indicates interest and engagement, whereas leaning backward can suggest disinterest or discomfort. Subtle shifts in posture during a conversation can reveal a shift in attitude or a response to specific information. Paying close attention to these changes is crucial in deciphering the subtle nuances of nonverbal communication.

Mirroring is another significant aspect of body language, often a subconscious reflection of rapport and connection. When two people are comfortable and connected, they may unconsciously mirror each other's posture, gestures, and even facial expressions. This mirroring can be a subtle indication of positive interaction and shared understanding. However, it's important to note that mirroring can be a conscious technique utilized by some individuals to build rapport or appear more likable. Recognizing the context and observing other nonverbal cues is crucial in determining whether mirroring is genuine or manipulative.

The interplay between hand gestures and posture creates a rich tapestry of nonverbal communication. A confident person might display open posture and assertive hand gestures, while a nervous individual might exhibit closed posture and frequent self-touching. It's crucial not to rely on a single gesture or posture in isolation; instead, focus on the combination and consistency of various nonverbal cues to obtain a more accurate and comprehensive interpretation.

The context is also paramount: A person might adopt a closed posture due to cold temperature, not necessarily because they are feeling defensive or uncomfortable.

In conclusion, mastering the interpretation of hand gestures and body posture is a powerful skill that enhances our ability to understand human behavior and build stronger, more meaningful relationships. By carefully observing these nonverbal cues and considering the overall context, we can unlock a wealth of information that often remains hidden beneath the surface of verbal communication. Remember, this is not about manipulating others but about cultivating a deeper understanding of human interaction and fostering more authentic connections. Through dedicated practice and mindful observation, you can significantly improve your ability to read people and navigate social situations with greater confidence and insight.

THE HOLISTIC APPROACH

Integrating verbal and nonverbal cues is not simply about adding two separate skill sets; it's about creating a holistic understanding of communication. Consider it like assembling a complex puzzle: individual pieces (verbal statements, facial expressions, posture, hand gestures) are meaningless on their own, but when put together, they reveal a complete picture. This picture is far richer and more
accurate than any single element could ever provide. This process involves recognizing the interplay between spoken words and unspoken signals, and understanding how these elements work together – or sometimes, work against each other – to convey meaning.

The concept of congruency versus incongruency is fundamental to this approach. Congruency refers to a situation where verbal and nonverbal messages align; what a person says matches their body language. For example, if someone says, "I'm thrilled about this opportunity," and their face lights up with a genuine smile, their body leans forward, and their hands are open and expressive, we can confidently interpret their message as sincere enthusiasm. The verbal and nonverbal cues reinforce each other, creating a powerful and believable message.

However, incongruency arises when there's a mismatch between verbal and nonverbal signals. This is where the real detective work begins. Imagine someone saying, "I'm fine," while simultaneously avoiding eye contact, fidgeting nervously, and clenching their jaw. The verbal message contradicts the nonverbal cues, suggesting a possible discrepancy between what the person is saying and how they truly feel. The incongruency signals that something might be amiss, potentially indicating discomfort, deception, or hidden emotions.

Identifying incongruencies requires keen observation and an understanding of context. A slight furrow of the brow, a fleeting microexpression of sadness, or a subtle shift in posture might be easily missed by a casual observer. However, for someone trained in recognizing nonverbal cues, these subtle signals can be invaluable in uncovering hidden meanings. The context is crucial here. What might be considered a normal fidget for one person could indicate nervousness or deception for another, depending on their baseline behavior and the situation. A person who habitually avoids eye contact might still be telling the truth; it is the *change* from their baseline that is often most revealing.

Developing the ability to detect incongruencies requires practice and self-awareness. Start by paying attention to your own body language. When you're feeling stressed, what are your nonverbal cues? When you're genuinely happy, how does your body express it? Understanding your own nonverbal communication will improve your ability to interpret the nonverbal communication of others. Practice observing people in different settings – a business meeting, a casual conversation, a family gathering – and note the discrepancies between their words and their actions.

One effective technique is to focus on specific nonverbal cues associated with deception or discomfort. These might include:

Microexpressions:
These are fleeting facial expressions that reveal true emotions, often lasting only a fraction of a second. Learning to recognize these requires dedicated practice and training, often through specialized courses or videos. A slight flicker of disgust, a momentary flash of fear, or a brief tightening of the lips can be highly revealing.

Eye Contact:
While direct eye contact is generally seen as a positive sign, excessive eye contact can be just as telling. Similarly, prolonged avoidance of eye contact could suggest deception or discomfort. Again, context is key. A person who is shy or introverted may naturally avoid eye contact, while someone who is lying might try to appear too confident and maintain excessive eye contact.

Posture:
A slumped posture might indicate low confidence or sadness, while a rigid, tense posture can be a sign of defensiveness or anxiety. An open, relaxed

posture often signifies comfort and openness.

Hand Gestures:
Manipulating objects, touching the face, or covering the mouth are often associated with deception or nervousness. However, it's important to note that these behaviors can also be associated with other emotions or simply habitual nervous tics.

Once you have observed potential incongruencies, it is essential to avoid jumping to conclusions. Instead, consider the overall context of the communication. What is the setting? What is the relationship between the people involved? What is the purpose of the communication? This broader perspective will help you interpret the nonverbal cues more accurately and avoid misinterpretations.

Furthermore, the holistic approach emphasizes the importance of considering the totality of the communication rather than focusing on individual cues in isolation. A single nonverbal cue may not necessarily indicate deception; rather, it is the clustering of nonverbal behaviors, combined with the verbal message, that provides a more accurate and complete interpretation.

For example, someone claiming they didn't break a vase might exhibit a fleeting microexpression of guilt, avoid direct eye contact, and fidget with their hands. While each cue individually might be open to interpretation, taken together, they paint a more convincing picture of deception.
Conversely, a single nonverbal cue, like avoiding eye contact, should not be interpreted as automatically

indicative of dishonesty. Context is critical. A person might avoid eye contact due to shyness, cultural norms, or even simply a distraction.

Building your skill in reading nonverbal communication is not simply about learning a set of rules; it is about cultivating a mindful, attentive approach to human interaction. It's about becoming a keen observer of the subtle nuances of human expression. Think of it as honing your perceptual acuity, expanding your awareness of the rich tapestry of human communication that goes beyond the spoken word. The more you practice, the more attuned you will become to these subtle signals, and the more accurate your interpretations will be. This is a skill that develops over time with consistent effort and attention to detail.

Ultimately, mastering the integration of verbal and nonverbal cues isn't about becoming a mind-reader; it's about enhancing your understanding of human communication and improving your ability to build stronger, more authentic relationships. By paying attention to both the spoken word and the unspoken signals, you gain a deeper insight into the true intentions and emotions of others, leading to more effective communication, improved decision-making, and richer, more fulfilling connections with those around you. Remember that this is a journey of continuous learning and improvement, requiring consistent practice and self-reflection to refine your skills. The more observant and perceptive you become, the more adept you will be at navigating the complex world of human interaction. This process allows you to decipher truth from deception, to build trust and understanding, and to navigate the intricacies of social dynamics with greater confidence and ease. It empowers you to unlock a deeper layer of communication, enabling you to interact more effectively and authentically in all aspects of life. By combining these skills, you'll become a more perceptive and intuitive communicator, enhancing your personal and professional relationships in significant ways.

This skill enables more nuanced comprehension of interactions, leading to greater success in various areas of life, from personal relationships to business negotiations. The ability to integrate verbal and nonverbal cues accurately is a valuable asset in nearly every facet of human interaction, significantly enhancing your ability to understand and
connect with others on a deeper level.

DEVELOPING KEEN OBSERVATIONAL SKILLS

Developing keen observational skills is the cornerstone of effectively reading people. It's not about passively watching; it's about actively engaging all your senses and focusing your attention to glean meaningful information from the seemingly insignificant details. This requires training your mind to become a highly attuned instrument, capable of picking up on subtle shifts in behavior that most people miss. Think of it like learning to hear the faintest whisper amidst a cacophony of noise.

The first step in developing this skill is cultivating mindful awareness. This involves consciously directing your attention to your surroundings and the people within them, without judgment or preconceived notions. Start by practicing simple exercises. For instance, spend five minutes observing a busy street scene. Don't try to analyze anything; simply observe. Note the clothing people are wearing, their gait, their interactions with each other. Notice the sounds, the smells, the overall atmosphere. This is a practice in clearing your mind and allowing yourself to absorb sensory information without filtering it. Repeat this exercise in different settings – a coffee shop, a park, a workplace – to expand your range of observation.

Another beneficial technique is to play observation games. These can be tailored to your interests and environment. For example, choose a specific object – a coffee cup, a tree, a person – and spend several minutes carefully observing its details. Note its shape, color, texture, any imperfections or unique features. Then, close your eyes and try to recreate a mental image of it, as precisely as possible. This exercise strengthens your ability to focus, retain, and recall details.

You can also try the "people-watching" game, which involves observing individuals in a public space and noting their behaviors without making any judgments. Try to guess their occupation, mood, or even their recent activities based solely on their appearance and demeanor. The goal isn't accuracy; it's about refining your observation skills and training your brain to notice details it might otherwise overlook.

Beyond these initial exercises, developing keen observational skills involves actively seeking opportunities to practice. Pay attention to details during conversations. Note not only the words being spoken but also the tone of voice, the pace of speech, and the accompanying body language. Observe facial expressions – not just the obvious ones, but the fleeting microexpressions that momentarily betray hidden emotions. Notice posture, hand gestures, and eye movements. Are the person's gestures congruent with their words? Do their eyes dart around nervously, or do they maintain consistent eye contact? These subtle inconsistencies often hold valuable clues.

The ability to observe effectively also hinges on minimizing distractions. In our increasingly busy and technology-driven world, this is a challenge. But by consciously creating
moments of quiet observation, we can train our brains to focus. Turn off your phone, find a quiet space, and deliberately observe your surroundings. This practice of mindfulness is not just beneficial for improving your
observation skills; it also promotes mental clarity and reduces stress.

Furthermore, understanding context is paramount. Where are you observing these individuals? What is the social setting?
What are the cultural norms? These contextual factors significantly influence how you interpret nonverbal cues. A gesture that might be considered polite in one culture could be offensive in another. Similarly, a seemingly aggressive posture might merely reflect someone's natural demeanor. By considering the context, you can avoid making inaccurate assumptions.

It's important to remember that observation is not about judging or labeling people. It's about understanding their behavior and motivations. Avoid preconceived notions and biases. Practice empathy, putting yourself in the other person's shoes to better understand their perspective. This approach fosters a more nuanced and accurate interpretation of their nonverbal communication.

To improve your observational skills even further, consider utilizing technology. For example, recording a conversation and then reviewing it slowly can reveal subtle details that were missed in real time. You can pause and rewind, paying close attention to microexpressions, shifts in posture, and other nonverbal cues. This allows for a more thorough and deliberate analysis of the communication. Video analysis, even of oneself, can provide a useful perspective on personal nonverbal communication habits. Watching videos of interactions – professional interviews, debates, or even casual conversations – can also be a valuable training tool.

Another advanced technique is to practice calibrating your observations. Calibration involves establishing a baseline of normal behavior for a specific individual. By observing someone in a neutral or relaxed setting, you can build a better understanding of their typical demeanor. Then, when you observe deviations from this baseline, you'll be better equipped to interpret their nonverbal cues. For example, if someone who is typically very expressive suddenly becomes withdrawn and quiet, it's a significant deviation that warrants further attention.

Practicing active listening is inextricably linked to keen observation. Active listening goes beyond simply hearing words; it involves actively engaging with the speaker and paying close attention to both their verbal and nonverbal cues. This includes maintaining eye contact, nodding to show you understand, and providing verbal affirmations like "I see" or "I understand." Active listening fosters rapport and creates a more open environment, making it easier to observe subtle nonverbal cues. It signals to the other person that you're genuinely interested and engaged, which often encourages more open and honest communication.

Furthermore, actively integrating verbal and nonverbal cues is crucial for a holistic understanding. Rarely does deception or true emotion reveal itself in a single gesture or statement. Instead, it often manifests as a cluster of inconsistencies, a mismatch between verbal and nonverbal signals. For example, someone might verbally claim to be happy, but their facial expression could betray a hint of sadness or anxiety. By carefully analyzing this cluster of cues, you can gain a more accurate insight into the person's true state of mind.

Mastering the art of observation is an ongoing process. It requires continuous practice, self-reflection, and a commitment to developing your awareness. The more you practice, the better you'll become at recognizing subtle cues and interpreting their meaning. It's a skill that applies to all aspects of life, from personal relationships to professional interactions. By honing your observational skills, you'll gain a deeper understanding of human behavior and enhance your ability to build stronger, more authentic connections with others. This skill enhances your ability to navigate social situations with greater confidence, make informed decisions, and live a more fulfilling life. The payoff for developing these skills extends far beyond simply "reading" people; it empowers you to better understand yourself and improve your overall communication efficacy.

Finally, remember that developing keen observational skills is not about trying to manipulate or deceive others. It is about gaining a deeper understanding of human interaction and communication. This knowledge can be used to build stronger relationships, improve your professional life, and navigate social situations with greater confidence and ease. Used ethically and responsibly, this heightened awareness is a powerful tool for personal and professional growth. The ultimate aim is not to outsmart or control but to better understand, empathize, and connect with others.

UNDERSTANDING CULTURAL NUANCES

Building upon the foundational skills of keen observation, we now delve into a crucial element often overlooked:
context. While mastering the art of noticing subtle shifts in body language, facial expressions, and posture is undeniably important, interpreting these cues accurately requires a profound understanding of their cultural context. Nonverbal communication, unlike spoken language, is not universally understood. Gestures, expressions, and even the concept of personal space vary significantly across cultures, and failing to account for these differences can lead to serious misunderstandings, misinterpretations, and even offense.

This section is dedicated to highlighting the critical importance of cultural sensitivity in the art of reading people.

Consider the simple act of a smile. In many Western cultures, a smile is generally interpreted as a sign of friendliness, happiness, or agreement. However, in some Asian cultures, a smile can be a way to mask discomfort, embarrassment, or even anger. A smile, therefore, in certain cultural contexts, might not indicate genuine positivity.

Similarly, eye contact, which is often considered a sign of engagement and honesty in Western societies, can be perceived as disrespectful or aggressive in other cultures. In some cultures, avoiding direct eye contact is a sign of respect and deference, particularly when interacting with elders or authority figures. Misinterpreting these cultural nuances could severely damage relationships and hinder effective communication.

The concept of personal space provides another excellent illustration of cultural variability. In many Western countries, people tend to maintain a relatively larger distance between themselves during conversations. Encroaching upon this personal space might be perceived as intrusive or even threatening. In contrast, some cultures have a much smaller concept of personal space, with closer proximity considered normal and acceptable during social interactions. A Westerner accustomed to a wider personal bubble might perceive someone from a culture with a smaller personal space as overly familiar or even aggressive, while the individual from the other culture might feel the Westerner is distant and unfriendly. This difference in personal space alone can greatly affect the interpretation of other nonverbal cues.

Gestures offer a rich tapestry of cultural differences. The "thumbs up" gesture, universally recognized as a sign of approval or encouragement in many Western countries, can be considered offensive in some Middle Eastern and Latin American cultures. Similarly, the "OK" sign, formed by joining the thumb and index finger to create a circle, is considered a gesture of friendship in many parts of the world, yet it is deeply offensive in some other cultures. Even seemingly innocent hand gestures, such as pointing, can carry vastly different connotations depending on the cultural context. In some cultures, pointing with a finger is considered rude, whereas in others, it is a perfectly acceptable way to direct someone's attention.

Beyond gestures and personal space, consider the impact of posture and body orientation. A relaxed posture, often interpreted as openness and confidence in some cultures, might be seen as a sign of disrespect or laziness in others. Similarly, the direction of one's body during a conversation can convey different meanings depending on the cultural context. In some cultures, maintaining direct body orientation towards the speaker demonstrates engagement and respect, while in others, a slightly angled posture might be considered more appropriate.

The interpretation of silence also varies significantly across cultures. In some cultures, silence is valued as a sign of respect and thoughtfulness, while in others, it might be interpreted as disinterest, disagreement, or even hostility.
Understanding these varying cultural attitudes towards silence is vital for accurate interpretation of nonverbal cues.

These examples underscore the critical need for

cultural awareness when interpreting nonverbal communication. Ignoring cultural context can lead to erroneous conclusions and hinder effective communication. To avoid these pitfalls, cultivate a habit of seeking information about the cultural background of the individuals you are observing. Conducting prior research, engaging in open-ended questions to gauge cultural understanding, and demonstrating genuine interest in the other person's background are crucial steps in developing cultural sensitivity.

Furthermore, recognize your own cultural biases. We all carry unconscious biases shaped by our upbringing and experiences, and these biases can subtly influence our interpretations of nonverbal cues. Being mindful of your own cultural lens and proactively challenging your assumptions is essential for accurate and unbiased observation. Actively seeking feedback from individuals from diverse cultural backgrounds can be invaluable in refining your understanding of cultural nuances in nonverbal communication.

The implications of neglecting cultural context extend beyond simple misunderstandings. In professional settings, misinterpreting nonverbal cues due to cultural differences can have significant consequences. Negotiations might fail, business deals might collapse, and professional relationships might be irreparably damaged due to inaccurate assessments based on culturally biased interpretations. In interpersonal relationships, such misinterpretations can strain friendships, damage romantic relationships, and hinder the development of trust and intimacy. In situations demanding empathy and understanding, such as healthcare or social work, culturally insensitive interpretations could lead to misdiagnosis, inadequate care, and a failure to provide appropriate support.

Developing cultural sensitivity is not merely a matter of politeness or political correctness; it is a crucial skill that enhances the accuracy and effectiveness of observation. It is about moving beyond superficial judgments based on limited understanding and towards a deeper appreciation of the diversity of human communication. By actively learning about different cultures, practicing empathy, and engaging in self-reflection, we can significantly improve our ability to interpret nonverbal cues accurately and ethically, thereby building stronger relationships and achieving better outcomes in all aspects of our lives.

To effectively navigate the complex landscape of intercultural communication, one needs to adopt a mindset of continuous learning and adaptation. This involves actively seeking opportunities to interact with individuals from
different cultural backgrounds, immersing oneself in diverse cultural experiences, and continually challenging personal assumptions and biases. One should actively seek out
educational resources, such as books, articles, and workshops, that provide deeper insights into cultural differences in nonverbal communication. Participating in cultural exchange programs or engaging with individuals from diverse backgrounds through social or professional

networks can also prove highly beneficial in this learning process.

In conclusion, while the ability to observe subtle nonverbal cues is a foundational skill in reading people, this skill is incomplete without a deep understanding of cultural context.

The meaning and interpretation of nonverbal cues vary significantly across cultures, highlighting the necessity of cultural awareness and sensitivity for effective and responsible observation. Ignoring cultural variations can lead to misinterpretations, misunderstandings, and ultimately, a failure to truly connect with and understand others. By acknowledging the importance of cultural nuances, actively seeking knowledge about different cultures, and remaining self-aware of one's own biases, one can enhance observational skills significantly, leading to more accurate interpretations, stronger relationships, and ultimately, a deeper understanding of the human experience. The journey of mastering the art of reading people is a lifelong pursuit, and incorporating cultural sensitivity forms an integral part of this continuous learning process. It is through this holistic approach that one can truly unlock the power of observation and harness its potential for personal and professional growth. The development of this skill requires continuous effort, self-reflection, and a commitment to learning and adapting throughout one's life. Only through this approach can we approach the art of reading people with accuracy, empathy, and respect.

OVERCOMING BIASES AND ASSUMPTIONS

Building on our understanding of cultural context, we now turn to another crucial aspect of mastering observation: overcoming our inherent biases and assumptions. We are all susceptible to biases, ingrained patterns of thinking that unconsciously shape our perceptions and interpretations.

These biases, often operating at a subconscious level, can significantly distort our readings of nonverbal cues, leading to inaccurate conclusions and potentially damaging misunderstandings. Understanding these biases and developing strategies to mitigate their influence is paramount to becoming a truly perceptive observer.

One of the most prevalent biases is confirmation bias, the tendency to favor information that confirms pre-existing beliefs and to disregard information that contradicts them.

Imagine, for instance, you're meeting someone for a business negotiation. If you've already formed a negative opinion about this person based on hearsay, you might unconsciously interpret their body language in a negative light, even if their actual cues suggest otherwise. A slight frown might be perceived as hostility rather than simple concentration, a relaxed posture as disinterest rather than composure. Confirmation bias essentially filters incoming information through the lens of your pre-conceived notions, leading to a skewed and ultimately inaccurate interpretation.

Another significant bias is the halo effect, where a single positive trait unduly influences our overall perception of an individual. If someone is exceptionally attractive, for
example, we might unconsciously attribute other positive qualities to them, such as intelligence or trustworthiness, even in the absence of supporting evidence. Conversely, the horn effect works in reverse: one negative trait overshadows all others, leading to an unfairly negative overall impression.
Someone who is perceived as unkempt might be automatically judged as unreliable or incompetent, regardless of their actual skills or abilities. These effects highlight how a single, often superficial, observation can warp our judgment of a multitude of other cues.

The availability heuristic plays a significant role as well. This cognitive shortcut involves relying on readily available information, even if it's not representative of the bigger picture. For example, if you've recently watched a
documentary on deception, you might become overly sensitive to signs of lying, perceiving microexpressions of discomfort or fleeting glances as definitive proof of dishonesty. Your recent

exposure to this information has skewed your perception, making you more likely to interpret ambiguous cues as evidence of deception, neglecting other, potentially more reliable, indicators.

Anchoring bias involves over-reliance on the first piece of information received. In a negotiation, the initial offer can act as an anchor, affecting subsequent perceptions and judgments. If the opening bid is incredibly high, subsequent offers, even if reasonable, might be perceived as less favorable simply because they're anchored to that high initial number. Similarly, the initial impression of a person can act as an anchor, influencing the interpretation of all subsequent interactions. Breaking free from this initial anchor is key to forming unbiased judgments.

The fundamental attribution error involves overemphasizing personality traits to explain someone's behavior while underestimating situational factors. If someone is late for a meeting, we might quickly assume they are irresponsible or inconsiderate, ignoring potential factors like traffic congestion or unforeseen circumstances. Conversely, we might attribute our own lateness to situational factors ("heavy traffic"), while judging others' lateness based on their character. This error leads to simplistic and often inaccurate assessments of behavior.

Overcoming these biases requires conscious effort and self-awareness. First, we must acknowledge our susceptibility to them. Regular self-reflection

and mindfulness practices can help identify our ingrained biases and their influence on our observations. Practicing empathy—trying to understand another person's perspective—is another crucial step.
Consider the situational factors at play before jumping to conclusions based on a limited set of cues.

Active listening and seeking clarification can mitigate the effects of bias. Instead of passively observing and interpreting nonverbal cues, engage in active listening, asking questions to clarify ambiguous observations and gain additional information. This open-ended approach minimizes reliance on assumptions and fosters a more nuanced
understanding.

Challenging our assumptions is crucial. Consciously question your initial interpretations. Are your interpretations based on solid evidence or mere speculation? What other explanations might account for the observed cues? By engaging in a process of continuous questioning and scrutiny, we can refine our assessments and reduce the impact of biases.

Cross-checking observations with other sources of information is essential. Don't rely solely on nonverbal cues; incorporate verbal communication, contextual information, and, where possible, input from other observers. This multi-faceted approach can help to confirm or challenge your initial interpretations, creating a more comprehensive understanding.

Moreover, keeping a journal to document your observations and reflections can be exceptionally beneficial. Note not only the nonverbal cues observed but also the context, your initial interpretations, and any subsequent corrections or adjustments. This practice allows for a systematic review of your interpretations and helps identify patterns of bias or misinterpretation over time. By regularly reviewing and analyzing these records, you'll identify areas where your biases are most likely to influence your judgments.

Furthermore, seeking feedback from trusted individuals can help identify blind spots and improve observational accuracy. Share your observations with someone you trust, explaining the reasoning behind your interpretations. Their perspective may reveal biases or inconsistencies you've overlooked. This feedback loop fosters continuous
improvement and reinforces the importance of critical self-assessment.

Finally, continuous learning and education are vital. Staying abreast of the latest research on body language, psychology, and cognitive biases expands our understanding of the
complexities of human behavior and enhances our ability to interpret nonverbal cues more accurately. Exposure to diverse perspectives and cultures further reduces our reliance on narrow, biased viewpoints.

The journey to mastering observation is a continuous process of refinement, self-reflection,

and learning. By acknowledging our inherent biases and employing the strategies discussed here, we can significantly improve our ability to interpret nonverbal cues accurately, building stronger relationships and making more informed decisions in all aspects of life. It's not about eliminating biases
entirely, an impossible task, but rather about minimizing their influence and developing a more nuanced, empathetic, and responsible approach to reading people. The commitment to this continuous process of self-improvement is what distinguishes a truly skilled observer from someone who simply relies on gut feelings and assumptions.

ACTIVE LISTENING AND EMPATHETIC OBSERVATION

Having laid the groundwork for mindful observation by addressing the pitfalls of inherent biases, we now delve into a crucial skill that amplifies our observational abilities: active listening. Active listening isn't merely hearing words; it's a conscious, multifaceted engagement with the speaker, encompassing verbal and nonverbal cues. It's about creating a safe space for genuine communication, fostering trust, and uncovering layers of meaning beyond the spoken word. When we actively listen, we are not just passively receiving information; we are actively participating in the construction of understanding. This active participation dramatically enhances our observational capacity.

Consider the scenario of a job interview. The candidate answers questions with seemingly confident verbal responses. However, a passive listener might only focus on the words, missing the subtle tremor in their voice when discussing a past failure or the nervous fidgeting of their hands. An active listener, on the other hand, would notice these nonverbal cues, understanding that they provide a richer, more nuanced picture of the candidate's true confidence level and resilience. The verbal content provides a framework, but the nonverbal signals often reveal the unspoken truth.

The key to active listening lies in creating an environment of genuine connection. Nonverbal cues are critical in this process. Maintaining appropriate eye contact, demonstrating an open and relaxed posture (avoiding crossed arms or legs, which can signal defensiveness), and subtly mirroring the speaker's posture (without being overtly imitative) can significantly improve the flow of communication. These subtle gestures communicate your engagement and encourage the speaker to open up further, revealing more through both their words and their body language.

Furthermore, active listening involves consciously focusing your attention on the speaker, minimizing internal distractions, and resisting the urge to formulate your response while they are still speaking. This requires discipline and practice. Our minds are often preoccupied with our own thoughts, anxieties, or plans for the future. To truly listen actively, we must consciously bring our focus back to the speaker, acknowledging the importance of their perspective and experience.

Effective active listening necessitates a conscious effort to understand not just the content of the message, but also the emotional context. This requires empathy – the ability to step into the speaker's shoes and understand their perspective from their frame of reference. Empathy isn't about agreeing with everything the speaker says; it's about understanding their feelings and motivations, even if you disagree with their conclusions. This empathetic understanding is crucial for accurately interpreting nonverbal cues, as emotions often manifest themselves subtly in body language.

Several techniques can enhance our active listening skills.One powerful technique is paraphrasing. This involves restating the speaker's message in your own words, ensuring you have accurately understood their point. For instance, if someone says, "I'm feeling really overwhelmed at work lately," you might respond with something like, "So you're feeling stressed and burdened by your workload?" This not only confirms your understanding but also shows the speaker that you are actively engaged and invested in their conversation.

Another effective technique is reflecting feelings. This involves identifying and acknowledging the speaker's emotions. If someone describes a frustrating experience, you might respond by saying, "That sounds incredibly
frustrating. I can understand why you'd be upset." This demonstrates empathy and validates the speaker's emotions, creating a safe space for further communication. It's crucial to be genuine in expressing empathy; insincere attempts can be easily detected and can damage trust.

Open-ended questions are also invaluable tools for active listening. These types of questions, unlike yes/no questions, encourage the speaker to elaborate on their thoughts and feelings. Instead of asking, "Are you stressed?", try asking, "Tell me more about how you're feeling at work." This prompts a more detailed response, revealing more information and providing a richer context for observation. By using open-ended questions, we encourage the speaker to share more deeply, unveiling subtle nonverbal cues that would otherwise remain hidden.

Beyond verbal techniques, mastering empathetic observation involves paying close attention to nonverbal cues. While actively listening to the speaker's words, simultaneously observe their body language. Are their hands tense? Do they avoid eye contact? Is their posture slumped or upright?
These nonverbal cues often reveal emotions and thoughts that aren't explicitly stated. For example, someone might verbally express confidence, but their fidgeting hands and averted gaze could contradict this verbal assertion, revealing underlying nervousness or insecurity.

The ability to integrate verbal and nonverbal cues is crucial for accurate interpretation. Consider a situation where someone tells you they're "fine," but their voice is flat, their shoulders are slumped, and they avoid eye contact. The verbal message contradicts the nonverbal signals. In this scenario, the nonverbal cues are likely more truthful, suggesting underlying distress. Learning to discern these inconsistencies is a key element of mastering both active listening and empathetic observation.

Furthermore, the art of empathetic observation extends beyond simply identifying nonverbal cues; it involves interpreting them within the larger context of the situation.

Cultural differences can significantly influence body language. What might be considered a sign of disrespect in one culture could be perfectly acceptable in another.Understanding cultural nuances is crucial for avoiding misinterpretations and developing accurate readings of nonverbal communication.

Empathetic observation also involves recognizing that people's communication styles vary. Some individuals are naturally more expressive than others. Some cultures encourage open displays of emotion, while others value restraint. Therefore, it's important to calibrate your observations based on your understanding of the individual and their cultural background. Avoid making sweeping generalizations based on limited observations; instead, strive for a nuanced and individualized interpretation of nonverbal cues.

Practicing active listening and empathetic observation is an ongoing process, demanding continuous self-reflection and refinement. It requires patience, empathy, and a genuine interest in understanding others. By combining conscious listening with mindful observation of nonverbal cues, you will unlock a deeper understanding of human communication, fostering stronger relationships and improving your ability to navigate complex social situations with greater confidence and accuracy. The more you practice, the more attuned you will become to the subtle nuances of human interaction, transforming your ability to read people from a rudimentary skill into a sophisticated art. The rewards extend far beyond simply identifying deception; they encompass building genuine connections, resolving conflicts more effectively, and ultimately, living a richer, more fulfilling life.

The ability to effectively combine active listening and empathetic observation is the cornerstone of truly mastering the art of reading people. It's a skill that builds over time, demanding consistent practice and self-awareness. By consciously cultivating these abilities, you will not only improve your observational skills but also strengthen your interpersonal relationships, navigate social situations with greater confidence, and ultimately enhance your overall quality of life. Remember that this is a journey, not a destination. Embrace the continuous learning process, and you will reap the immense benefits of becoming a truly perceptive and empathetic observer. The journey of mastering observation is a lifelong endeavor, continuously evolving and deepening with every interaction.

THE IMPORTANCE OF CALIBRATION AND BASELINE BEHAVIOR

The cornerstone of accurate interpretation in reading people lies in establishing a reliable baseline of their behavior. Without this crucial first step, any subsequent observation of nonverbal cues risks misinterpretation. Think of it like attempting to diagnose a medical condition without a complete patient history; you might spot a symptom, but without understanding the individual's normal state, you can't confidently determine its significance. Similarly, observing someone's behavior in isolation, without a clear understanding of their typical demeanor, can lead to inaccurate, even misleading conclusions.

Establishing this baseline requires patient and attentive observation over time. It's not a quick process, and it demands a commitment to mindful observation, free from pre-conceived notions or biases. The goal is not to create a rigid profile, but rather a flexible understanding of an individual's typical presentation in different contexts. This understanding will inform your subsequent observations, providing a reliable yardstick against which to measure deviations.

Consider, for instance, a colleague known for their animated gestures and enthusiastic tone during team meetings. If, during a particular meeting, this colleague exhibits unusually subdued body language, minimal hand gestures, and a quieter tone of voice, it warrants closer attention. This deviation from their established baseline suggests something might be amiss—perhaps they are feeling stressed, uncertain, or even apprehensive about a particular project. Without knowing their usual behavior, you might misinterpret their quiet demeanor as disinterest or even hostility.

The process of establishing a baseline is particularly important when dealing with individuals you only interact with occasionally. In these instances, forming a comprehensive understanding of their baseline may take longer. It involves consciously paying attention to their posture, facial expressions, tone of voice, and overall demeanor in different settings. Observe their interactions with others, their responses to various stimuli, and their general behavior in relaxed situations. For example, if you're trying to assess the honesty of a potential business partner whom you've only met a few times, you need to carefully observe their demeanor in less formal settings before drawing conclusions about their behavior during negotiations.

Another crucial aspect is recognizing the influence of context on behavior. An individual's baseline may shift depending on the situation. A typically reserved person might be more expressive and animated in a social setting amongst close friends, while someone usually outgoing might appear more subdued in a formal business meeting.Recognizing these contextual variations is essential to avoiding misinterpretations. For example, a person might typically maintain strong eye contact, but in a situation involving a high level of authority, such as a police interrogation, they might avert their gaze, not necessarily as a sign of deceit but rather as a response to the inherent power dynamic. Therefore, context is a vital piece of the puzzle. Furthermore, understanding an individual's cultural background is also paramount in establishing a reliable

baseline. Nonverbal cues can vary significantly across cultures, and what might be considered normal in one culture could be interpreted differently in another. For example, prolonged eye contact can be seen as a sign of respect in some cultures, while in others, it can be perceived as a challenge or even aggression. Similarly, the interpretation of personal space varies considerably across cultures.

Awareness of these cultural nuances helps to prevent misjudgments rooted in cultural misunderstandings, ensuring that your interpretations are informed and accurate.

Moreover, the process of establishing a baseline isn't static; it's an ongoing process of refinement and adaptation. As your relationship with an individual evolves, your understanding of their baseline behavior will also evolve. You may observe subtle shifts in their demeanor over time, possibly influenced by life changes, new experiences, or evolving relationships. Being mindful of these shifts allows for a more nuanced and accurate understanding of the individual. For instance, a colleague who was previously always punctual and organized might experience a period of disorganization and tardiness due to personal issues.

Recognizing this shift in behavior, rather than assuming a change in personality, demonstrates empathy and understanding.

The importance of a reliable baseline also extends to the detection of deception. While there is no single, universally reliable indicator of lying, deviations from an established baseline can be significant clues. For example, if someone consistently maintains strong eye contact but suddenly avoids eye contact during a specific question, this deviation from their typical behavior might suggest discomfort or deception.

It's important to remember, however, that this is just one potential indicator among many, and it's crucial to consider the context and other nonverbal cues before reaching any conclusions. A sudden increase in nervous behaviors such as fidgeting or throat clearing, or changes in speech patterns like pauses or hesitations, could also be noteworthy deviations from their baseline.

However, it's equally important to avoid jumping to conclusions based solely on observed deviations from the baseline. A multitude of factors can influence behavior, including stress, fatigue, illness, or simply a bad day.

Therefore, a comprehensive analysis requires considering all available information and using multiple indicators to form a holistic and accurate interpretation. Relying on a single nonverbal cue to determine deception or other internal states is unreliable and prone to error.

Consider the case of someone who is typically very open and expressive in their communication style, but who during a crucial conversation suddenly becomes more reserved and hesitant. Without the baseline, you might interpret this immediately as a sign of deception. However, considering their baseline, the shift in their behavior might simply signify nervousness or anxiety associated with the high-stakes conversation.

The process of calibrating your observations and understanding baseline behavior is continuous and requires practice. The more you practice, the more adept you will become at identifying and interpreting subtle deviations from the norm. This skill enhances your ability to not only detect deception, but also understand emotional states, build empathy, and ultimately, build stronger and more meaningful relationships. It's a dynamic skill that strengthens with every interaction and observation, refining your ability to
accurately interpret human behavior. By developing this skill, you move beyond simply observing to truly understanding the unspoken language that pervades our daily interactions. This sophisticated understanding then allows you to respond to individuals more thoughtfully, and to construct more meaningful and empathetic communication.

The mastery of observation isn't merely about spotting inconsistencies or identifying deceptive behavior; it's about developing a deep understanding of the individual you're observing, appreciating the context of their behavior, and appreciating the complexity of human interaction.

Remember, context is king. Understanding the situation, the individuals involved, and the cultural nuances plays a critical role in interpreting nonverbal cues accurately. By focusing on the complete picture, and integrating your observations with your knowledge of baseline behavior, you transform from a passive observer to an active and insightful interpreter of human communication. This process ultimately fosters more meaningful connections and allows you to engage in more productive and fulfilling relationships, both professionally and personally. The ongoing practice of calibration and the development of a keen understanding of baseline behavior are fundamental to mastering the art of observation and unlocking a deeper understanding of the human experience.

VERBAL AND NONVERBAL CLUES

Deception, a universal human behavior, often leaves subtle traces in our communication. While words may attempt to mask the truth, our bodies often betray our intentions through a complex interplay of verbal and nonverbal cues. Mastering the art of detecting deception requires a keen eye for detail, an understanding of human psychology, and a healthy dose of skepticism. This chapter will equip you with the tools to decipher these subtle signs, allowing you to navigate the complexities of human interaction with greater confidence and awareness.

One of the most significant indicators of deception lies in the inconsistencies between verbal and nonverbal messages. A person's words might claim innocence, but their body
language may tell a different story. For example, someone denying involvement in an incident might maintain steady eye contact, but simultaneously fidget with their hands or shift their weight repeatedly. This incongruence, the mismatch between what's being said and what's being communicated nonverbally, often signals deception. The more pronounced this incongruence, the stronger the suspicion.

Let's delve into the realm of nonverbal cues associated with deception. While no single gesture definitively proves a lie, clusters of behaviors frequently emerge. Consider these common nonverbal indicators:

Microexpressions:
These fleeting, involuntary facial expressions reveal true emotions, often contradicting consciously controlled verbal statements. A fleeting look of guilt or fear, lasting only a fraction of a second, might betray a lie despite a calm, composed demeanor. Mastering the recognition of microexpressions requires practice and a keen understanding of facial musculature and emotional responses. Repeated viewings of videos illustrating microexpressions, slowing down the footage, can significantly enhance your ability to detect them.

Eye Contact:
While prolonged eye contact can sometimes signal confidence, an avoidance of eye contact is often associated with deception, especially in cultures where direct eye contact is considered polite and respectful. However, remember cultural nuances; in some cultures, avoiding eye contact is a sign of respect, not necessarily deception. The key is not to focus solely on the presence or absence of eye contact, but on changes in eye contact patterns, particularly sudden avoidance or excessive staring. Consider the baseline; what is the individual's normal eye contact behavior before reaching a conclusion.

Body Language:

Shifts in posture, fidgeting, and self-touching behaviors (like touching the nose, ears, or neck) are often associated with discomfort and deception. These behaviors represent attempts to self-soothe or manage anxiety in stressful situations. A sudden stiffening of posture, or conversely, a slumping of the shoulders, might indicate stress or discomfort related to the subject at hand. The intensity and frequency of these actions provide further insight; repeated nervous twitches are more significant than a single, isolated gesture.

Vocal Cues:
Changes in tone, pitch, and speech rate are also important indicators. A hesitant or stammering response, an unusually high-pitched voice, or a sudden change in speech volume can indicate stress or deception. Similarly, pauses and hesitations, particularly if uncharacteristic of the person's normal speech patterns, might suggest that the individual is struggling to formulate a believable lie.

Incongruent Gestures:
Observe if a person's hand gestures are consistent with their words. For example, someone describing a large object might use small, insignificant hand gestures, raising suspicion. Similarly, a lack of illustrative gestures when narrating a detailed event is uncommon and may indicate dishonesty.

Beyond individual cues, it is crucial to understand the significance of *clusters* of nonverbal behavior. A single fidgety gesture doesn't necessarily indicate deception, but when combined with inconsistent eye contact, microexpressions of guilt, and inconsistent verbal statements, the likelihood of deception increases substantially. It's the convergence of multiple cues that paints a more comprehensive picture.

To effectively analyze nonverbal cues, one must carefully establish a *baseline.* Observe the person's typical behavior in a relaxed, comfortable setting before entering the situation where deception might occur. This baseline establishes a norm against which to compare subsequent behavior. Deviations from this baseline—sudden changes in eye contact, posture, or speech patterns—become much more significant. This comparative analysis is crucial for accurate interpretation.

Let's illustrate with a few scenarios:

Scenario 1:
A job applicant is asked about a gap in their resume. They provide a plausible explanation, but simultaneously touch their nose repeatedly, avoid eye contact, and their voice trembles slightly. This cluster of nonverbal behaviors raises significant doubt, suggesting possible deception.

Scenario 2:
A suspect is questioned about a theft. They vehemently deny involvement, maintaining steady eye contact but exhibiting excessive sweating, rapid breathing, and fidgeting with their hands throughout the interrogation. Again, this cluster of nonverbal cues raises significant suspicion.

Scenario 3:
During a casual conversation, a friend mentions a recent trip, describing a luxurious hotel stay but exhibiting little enthusiasm, using minimal hand gestures, and avoiding prolonged eye contact. These cues, in context, suggest possible exaggeration or falsehood about the trip's details.

However, it is vital to remember that nonverbal cues are not foolproof. Cultural variations, individual differences in personality and expression, and genuine nervousness can all mimic signs of deception. Therefore, it's essential to consider the context and to avoid jumping to conclusions based on isolated cues. Interpretation always requires a holistic
approach, considering both verbal and nonverbal communication in its entirety.

Furthermore, ethical considerations are paramount. The knowledge you gain from studying deception detection should never be used to manipulate or exploit others.
Instead, it serves as a tool for improving communication, enhancing your ability to assess situations accurately, and building stronger, more trusting relationships. Respect for individual privacy and avoiding judgments based solely on nonverbal cues are fundamental to the responsible application of these techniques. Never mistake observational skills for a truth serum; instead, employ your improved understanding to navigate relationships more effectively.

Mastering the art of reading people requires ongoing practice and refinement. By constantly observing and analyzing behavior, you will sharpen your observational skills and enhance your ability to interpret nonverbal cues accurately.

Continual learning, and self-reflection on your own interpretations are crucial for consistent improvement. As you gain experience, you'll develop a more intuitive understanding of the subtle signals that communicate truth and falsehood. This chapter has offered a foundation; your ongoing practice will build your expertise. Remember, the objective is not to become a lie detector, but to gain a deeper understanding of human communication and the often subtle ways we reveal our true selves.

ANALYZING CLUSTERS OF NONVERBAL CUES

Analyzing individual nonverbal cues can be misleading. A single fidgeting hand, a fleeting glance away, or a slight hesitation in speech doesn't automatically equate to deception. Experienced deceivers often meticulously control individual behaviors. The key to accurate deception detection lies in recognizing *clusters* of nonverbal cues—patterns of inconsistencies between verbal and nonverbal communication, and inconsistencies within the nonverbal behavior itself. This synergistic approach significantly increases the reliability of your assessment.

Consider a scenario where you're questioning someone about a missing item. They verbally deny any involvement, yet their hands remain clasped tightly together—a potential indicator of anxiety or concealed information. Taken alone, the clasped hands might be interpreted in various ways: nervousness about the situation generally, cold hands, or simply a habitual gesture. However, if this is coupled with several other cues—a noticeably increased blink rate, avoiding direct eye contact, and a slightly higher-pitched voice than usual—the picture shifts. The cluster of cues, taken together, creates a more compelling case for possible deception than any single element in isolation.

Let's dissect this concept further. A cluster of nonverbal cues demonstrating potential deception often features these interconnected elements:

Inconsistency between verbal and nonverbal communication:
This is perhaps the most critical indicator. Someone saying "I'm completely relaxed" while exhibiting visibly tense shoulders, rapid breathing, and sweaty palms presents a clear discrepancy. The verbal message contradicts the nonverbal signals, raising a red flag. This discrepancy is crucial because it showcases a lack of congruence – a hallmark of potential deception. The individual is consciously trying to control their words, but their body is leaking the truth. The greater the discrepancy, the stronger the indication of deception.

Changes in baseline behavior:
Everyone has a baseline of normal nonverbal behavior. A naturally fidgety person might show more fidgeting when telling a lie, but the increase in *fidgeting, beyond their typical baseline, becomes a relevant indicator. Similarly, a usually talkative person suddenly becoming unusually quiet might suggest deception. It's the* change from their established behavior that should trigger further investigation. Analyzing this requires prior observation, perhaps a casual conversation to establish the individual's typical demeanor. This established baseline then serves as a crucial reference point for comparing subsequent behavior.

Microexpressions:

These are fleeting facial expressions, lasting only fractions of a second, that betray true emotions. A brief flash of fear or disgust, quickly masked by a smile, could indicate suppressed negative feelings related to the subject at hand. Detecting microexpressions requires keen observation and practice, but mastering this skill provides invaluable insights into hidden emotions. It's not about simply seeing the microexpression itself, but understanding its context within the larger cluster of nonverbal cues.

Body language clusters related to specific emotions: Certain clusters of nonverbal cues are frequently associated with specific emotions commonly experienced when
deceiving someone. For example, a cluster of anxiety might include rapid breathing, increased heart rate, sweaty palms, fidgeting, avoidance of eye contact, and speech hesitations. These cues, in combination, suggest a far greater likelihood of deception than any of them alone. Understanding the relationship between specific emotions and their nonverbal manifestations is paramount in detecting deception.

Patterns over time:
Deception often isn't a single event; it's a process. Analyzing a series of interactions with an individual allows you to observe consistent patterns in their behavior. Suppose you observe someone exhibiting a cluster of nervous behaviors whenever a specific topic arises. Over several interactions, this repeated pattern reinforces the likelihood that they are concealing something related to that topic. This emphasis on patterns

underscores the importance of observing multiple interactions instead of relying solely on a single encounter.

Let's illustrate this with a real-life example. Imagine you're conducting a job interview. A candidate answers a question about their previous employment, stating they left on good terms. Their verbal response is positive and professional. However, observe these nonverbal cues: they avoid eye contact momentarily, then quickly glance downwards before returning their gaze; their shoulders tense slightly and they briefly touch their nose. This small cluster of cues, inconsistent with their positive verbal response, triggers further investigation. If, during the interview, these nonverbal behaviors repeatedly manifest whenever the past employment is discussed, the cluster of cues becomes more significant, indicating potential deception or at least significant discomfort with the topic. This might not be proof of lying, but it certainly warrants further, more detailed questioning, perhaps focusing on specific aspects of their previous role or departure.

To effectively analyze clusters of nonverbal cues, you must adopt a holistic approach. It's not simply a matter of ticking off individual cues on a checklist; it's about understanding the interplay between them. Consider the context of the situation, the individual's personality and baseline behavior, and the overall emotional tone of the interaction. The more cues converge, and the greater the incongruence between verbal and nonverbal communication, the stronger the indication of deception.

However, it's crucial to remember that observing nonverbal cues isn't foolproof. Numerous factors can influence an individual's behavior, including stress, fatigue, cultural differences, medical conditions, and personality traits.

Misinterpretations can easily occur if you lack sufficient context and experience. Consequently, avoid making definitive judgments based solely on nonverbal cues.
Instead, use them as valuable pieces of information to inform your overall assessment, prompting further investigation and clarification through open-ended questions and attentive listening. Remember, your goal isn't to definitively label someone as a liar but to gain a deeper understanding of the situation and the individual involved.

Furthermore, context is everything. What might be considered a deceptive cue in one situation could be perfectly innocent in another. A person avoiding eye contact might be shy, respectful of cultural norms, or simply suffering from eye fatigue. Similarly, fidgeting could stem from boredom, nervousness, or simply an individual's natural habit. Proper interpretation demands careful consideration of the surrounding circumstances.

Cultivating your ability to analyze clusters of nonverbal cues requires continuous practice and self-reflection. Start by observing people in everyday situations. Pay attention to the interplay between their words and actions. Consider the context, their baseline behavior, and the overall emotional tone. Practice identifying inconsistencies and interpreting clusters of cues.

Over time, you will develop a sharper eye for detail and a more nuanced understanding of nonverbal communication. This continuous learning will make you a more adept observer of human behavior and increase your ability to interpret the subtle nuances of human communication. Remember, becoming proficient in this skill takes time and dedication, but the rewards – improved communication and stronger relationships – are invaluable.

The goal is not to become a lie detector, but a more perceptive and empathetic observer of human behavior, capable of navigating social situations with enhanced awareness and confidence.

MICROEXPRESSIONS AND DECEPTION

The human face, a canvas of emotions, often reveals more than words can express. While conscious attempts at deception might manifest in carefully crafted narratives and controlled body language, our subconscious leaks
information through microexpressions – fleeting, involuntary facial expressions that betray our true feelings. These are the telltale signs of deception, often lasting only a fraction of a second, yet carrying significant weight in unraveling the truth. They are the involuntary muscle movements that contradict the carefully constructed facade. Understanding microexpressions is not about becoming a cynical skeptic, constantly questioning everyone's honesty. Instead, it's about honing a skill to better understand the complex interplay of human communication.

Paul Ekman, a pioneer in the field of microexpressions, has dedicated his life to researching and cataloging these subtle shifts in facial expressions. His work demonstrates that certain fundamental emotions – happiness, sadness, anger, fear, surprise, disgust, and contempt – manifest universally through distinct microexpressions. While cultural norms might influence the display of emotions, the underlying muscular movements remain largely consistent across cultures. This universality provides a foundation for recognizing these expressions, regardless of a person's background or social conditioning.

Recognizing microexpressions isn't merely about passively observing a face; it demands active engagement. It requires training your eyes to identify the subtle nuances—the rapid contraction of a muscle around the eye, a fleeting tightening of the lips, a barely perceptible furrow of the brow. These are not the exaggerated expressions we often see in theatre or cartoons; they are much more subtle, often barely noticeable to the untrained eye. This is where diligent practice becomes paramount.

Consider this scenario: You're interviewing a candidate for a highly competitive position. During the interview, the candidate articulates their impressive qualifications and experience with remarkable confidence. However, as they describe a past accomplishment, a flicker of a microexpression crosses their face – a fleeting flash of fear or disgust, perhaps. This subtle expression, lasting only a fraction of a second, might contradict their confident verbal delivery. This subtle inconsistency between their words and their microexpressions raises a red flag, suggesting a possible discrepancy in their narrative. It's essential to acknowledge that this doesn't automatically confirm deception, but it does warrant further investigation. It prompts you to delve deeper into their claims, perhaps asking more specific questions to uncover the potential truth behind the conflicting cues.

Developing the skill of identifying microexpressions demands consistent practice. Start by watching videos specifically designed for microexpression training. Several videos and online resources showcase various expressions, each with their corresponding emotion. This visual training enhances your ability to discern the subtle differences between expressions. Pay close attention to the speed at which the expressions appear and disappear; this ephemeral nature is their hallmark. Don't expect to master this overnight. The key is consistent practice and repetition. The more you engage with this training, the more adept you become at identifying these fleeting indicators.

After familiarizing yourself with the basic microexpressions, move onto real-life practice. This isn't about scrutinizing every face you encounter; rather, it involves paying mindful attention during conversations and interactions. Observe the interplay between verbal and nonverbal communication. Do the words match the expressions? Are there subtle inconsistencies that require further attention? Begin by focusing on a single emotion at a time. For example, start by practicing recognition of fear, concentrating on the specific muscle movements associated with it – widened eyes, raised eyebrows, and possibly slightly parted lips.

Once you feel comfortable identifying a single microexpression, expand your focus to encompass multiple emotions. Observe how microexpressions can combine or overlap, creating complex blends of emotions. A person might exhibit a flash of anger immediately followed by a fleeting attempt at masking it with a forced smile. This blend reveals a more nuanced emotional landscape, one that wouldn't be apparent through mere verbal analysis.

This process of observation and analysis should be systematic, and not judgmental. Remember, you're not aiming to label someone as a liar; instead, you're attempting to gain a more profound understanding of their emotional state. The goal isn't to condemn, but to understand. This nuanced approach makes you a more empathetic observer, capable of navigating complex social interactions with increased sensitivity and awareness.

Beyond recognizing the isolated microexpressions, pay close attention to the context. The same microexpression can mean different things depending on the situation. For example, a brief flash of fear might be a natural reaction to a loud noise, while the same expression during a seemingly insignificant conversation might suggest deception or concealment.

Consider the person's baseline behavior – how do they typically express themselves? What are their usual facial expressions and body language? Comparing the observed behavior with their baseline helps you determine if a microexpression is genuinely an unusual reaction or simply part of their standard expression repertoire.

Consider the sequence of microexpressions. A

quick succession of anger, fear, and then a forced smile indicates a struggle to maintain control over emotions. This sequence, observed in conjunction with incongruent verbal statements, strongly suggests deception. The layering of microexpressions reveals a deeper emotional complexity, going beyond the simple reading of individual expressions.

Another crucial aspect is considering the person's overall demeanor. Does their body language align with their verbal message and facial expressions? Inconsistencies between posture, hand gestures, and microexpressions can further support the identification of deception. For instance, someone might verbally deny involvement in an incident, yet their shoulders may be hunched, their hands fidgeting nervously, while a microexpression of guilt briefly flickers across their face. The cluster of these nonverbal cues, when combined with the incongruence of their verbal response, paints a more comprehensive picture.

Practice interpreting these clusters of cues. The more experience you gain, the more easily you'll recognize subtle incongruities and inconsistencies. However, remember that microexpressions alone don't definitively prove deception. They offer valuable insights, prompting further investigation and a more nuanced understanding of the person's emotional landscape. They are pieces of a puzzle, not the entire solution.Beyond recognizing microexpressions, consider the context and cultural background of the person you are observing.

Certain microexpressions can be misinterpreted if cultural norms are not considered. For example, a slight downturn of the mouth might signify sadness in one culture, while
representing a thoughtful expression in another. Understanding these cultural nuances enhances the accuracy of your observation and prevents misinterpretations.
Researching common cultural expressions and body language cues will refine your observations, avoiding potentially inaccurate assumptions.

Furthermore, keep in mind that expertise in microexpression analysis is not about becoming a 'lie detector.' The goal is to become a more insightful and empathetic observer of human behaviour, capable of picking up on subtle cues that might otherwise be missed. This deeper understanding enhances communication, fostering more genuine and trusting relationships. The aim is not to judge, but to understand, and thereby build stronger connections based on mutual respect and transparency. It's a skill that enhances personal and professional relationships, bringing a greater depth of
understanding to every interaction.

Continuous learning and observation are paramount in mastering the art of reading microexpressions. Regular practice, focusing on both isolated expressions and their combined effect within a context, is crucial to honing this skill. The more you engage with the nuances of human behavior, the more perceptive you will become, not only in spotting deception, but also in fostering deeper understanding and empathy in your interactions. Remember that this is a journey of continuous learning and refinement. The ability to accurately interpret microexpressions is a skill built over time through dedication, practice, and mindful observation. The rewards, however, are invaluable, leading to improved communication, stronger relationships, and a deeper understanding of the human experience.

QUESTIONING TECHNIQUES AND DECEPTION DETECTION

The ability to read microexpressions provides a powerful foundation in discerning truth from falsehood, but it's only one piece of the puzzle. Effective questioning techniques are crucial to complement your observational skills, drawing out further nonverbal cues and solidifying your assessment. The art of questioning is not about aggressive interrogation; rather, it's about strategically guiding the conversation to elicit truthful and consistent responses, revealing inconsistencies or evasiveness that might otherwise go unnoticed.

The first principle revolves around the type of questions you pose. Closed-ended questions, those requiring a simple "yes" or "no" answer, limit the opportunity for nonverbal
expression and offer little room for revealing inconsistencies.
They allow the subject to easily control their response, masking any underlying deception. For

instance, asking "Did you take the money?" provides a simple, easily manipulated answer. A deceptive individual can readily offer a "no" without significant nonverbal leakage.

In contrast, open-ended questions invite more detailed responses, providing a richer landscape for observing nonverbal cues. These questions encourage elaboration and spontaneous reactions, making it harder for someone to maintain a fabricated narrative. Instead of asking "Did you take the money?", try "Can you describe your actions yesterday afternoon?" or "Walk me through your routine after leaving the office." These inquiries demand more detailed explanations, allowing you to observe the subject's body language, tone of voice, and the consistency of their story. Inconsistencies between their verbal statements and their nonverbal cues – such as shifting eyes, fidgeting, or avoiding eye contact – might signal deception.

The power of open-ended questions lies not only in their ability to expose deception, but also in their ability to build rapport. By encouraging a more conversational approach, you create a more relaxed environment, which can sometimes lead to a more honest, less guarded response.
However, be mindful of the phrasing. Avoid leading questions that suggest a specific answer, unintentionally biasing the response. For instance, instead of "You were at the meeting, weren't you?", ask "What can you tell me about the meeting?" Subtle differences in phrasing can drastically alter the nature of the response and the information gleaned.

Beyond the type of question, consider the *sequence* of your questioning. Start with general, less threatening questions to establish a baseline of their normal behavior. Observe their baseline posture, eye contact, and speaking mannerisms. This baseline provides a crucial benchmark against which to compare subsequent responses to more probing questions.

As you move toward more sensitive topics, the contrast between their baseline behavior and their reactions to the more challenging questions will become more apparent.

Another key technique is to employ "repetition with variation." Ask the same question in multiple ways, slightly altering the wording or context. Inconsistent responses, even minor ones, may indicate deception. A person telling the truth will consistently narrate their story, regardless of how the question is phrased. A liar, however, is more likely to stumble or modify details in their narrative as they struggle to maintain a consistent falsehood. For example, after asking "Where were you last night?", you could later ask "Can you describe your evening activities?" or "Who did you spend time with last night?". Discrepancies in timing, locations, or individuals mentioned could be telltale signs of deception.

Furthermore, carefully observe the timing of their responses.
Unnecessary pauses or overly rapid answers can be revealing. A prolonged pause might indicate the subject is constructing a fabricated story, while excessively fast responses may reflect an attempt to

prevent themselves from being caught in a lie.

Analyzing the consistency of their verbal and nonverbal cues is paramount. Pay close attention to the congruency between their words and their body language. Do their facial
expressions match their statements? Does their posture reflect their purported emotions? Are their hand gestures natural and congruent with their words? Inconsistencies –such as a smile that doesn't reach the eyes, or a nervous fidgeting during a seemingly straightforward explanation – are often strong indicators of deception.

Beyond body language, consider the content of their responses. Are they providing excessively detailed information in an attempt to appear convincing? Or conversely, are they offering vague and evasive answers, avoiding specific details? Both extremes can be suspicious. A truthful person usually provides a level of detail commensurate with the question asked; they won't overcompensate with unnecessary details or resort to vague generalizations.

Finally, be mindful of contextual clues. Consider the overall situation, the subject's personality, and any prior knowledge you may have. This contextual understanding adds depth to your interpretation of their nonverbal cues. A person who is typically reserved might exhibit more pronounced nonverbal responses under stress, while a naturally expressive person might show subtler cues when deceptive. Understanding these nuances requires practice and observation of a variety of individuals in various settings.

Effective questioning and deception detection are intricate skills that require both theoretical understanding and practical application. It's not about identifying a single definitive sign, but about accumulating multiple indicators, observing patterns, and understanding the context. By combining the insightful observation of microexpressions with strategic questioning and a keen understanding of human behavior, you equip yourself with a powerful arsenal for uncovering the truth. Remember that this is a skill honed over time through consistent practice and mindful observation. The more experience you accumulate, the more adept you become at identifying deception and fostering trust in your interactions. This isn't about manipulating others; it's about empowering yourself to navigate the complexities of human communication with greater understanding and confidence. Develop your skills incrementally, always respecting the inherent complexities and nuances of human interaction, and remember that your goal is to understand, not judge. Your ability to discern truth will only become stronger with practice, patience and persistence.

The process is iterative. After asking a series of open-ended questions and observing the responses, you may need to revisit specific areas, asking clarifying questions or rephrasing to elicit more information. It's a conversation, not an interrogation. The goal is to gently guide the individual towards a more complete and accurate account of events, while remaining mindful of the potential for unintentional bias.

Remember that no single indicator definitively proves deception. The strength of your assessment rests on the accumulation of multiple, consistent indicators. A single fleeting microexpression, an isolated inconsistent statement, or a slightly hesitant pause is not enough on its own.

However, when several of these subtle cues converge, they paint a more compelling picture. Document your observations, noting the specific nonverbal cues, the content of the responses, and the context in which they occurred. This detailed record will assist in your analysis and provide support for your conclusions. This is crucial, especially in situations where the stakes are high or require rigorous evidence.

In conclusion, mastering the art of questioning and deception detection is a journey, not a destination. It requires continuous learning, diligent practice, and a deep understanding of both verbal and nonverbal communication. By combining the power of open-ended questions, mindful observation of body language and microexpressions, and a rigorous analysis of consistency, you significantly enhance your ability to penetrate the surface and gain a deeper understanding of the people and situations you encounter.

The rewards are significant, offering not only improved interpersonal skills but also a heightened capacity for accurate judgment and effective decision-making. This skill set is invaluable, applicable in various aspects of life – from personal relationships to professional negotiations and beyond.

ETHICAL CONSIDERATIONS IN DECEPTION DETECTION

The power to discern truth from deception, honed through the careful observation of body language and the strategic application of questioning techniques, carries with it a significant ethical responsibility. While the skills detailed in this book can be invaluable in various aspects of life, their application must always be guided by a strong moral
compass. Misinterpreting nonverbal cues, drawing hasty conclusions, or using this knowledge for manipulative purposes can have profound negative consequences,
undermining trust and harming relationships.

One of the most critical ethical considerations is respecting individual privacy. The ability to interpret subtle nonverbal signals provides a window into a person's internal world, exposing vulnerabilities and hidden emotions. It is crucial to remember that this insight is not a license for unwarranted intrusion. We must always be mindful of the context in which we observe and interpret behavior. Observing someone's nervous fidgeting in a high-pressure job interview, for example, is vastly different from observing similar behavior in a casual conversation. The same behavior can have vastly different meanings.

The temptation to make snap judgments based solely on nonverbal cues must be actively resisted. Body language provides valuable clues, but it is rarely, if ever, conclusive evidence of deception or any other internal state. A single gesture, facial expression, or postural shift, taken out of context, can be easily misinterpreted. Accurate interpretation requires a holistic understanding of the individual, the situation, and the surrounding circumstances. One must consider the person's cultural background, personality, and potential medical conditions, all of which can influence their nonverbal communication. For example, someone from a culture that values less direct eye contact might be
misinterpreted as being deceptive, when they are simply adhering to cultural norms.

Consider the implications of applying deception detection skills in professional settings. In negotiations, sales, or human resources, the temptation to use these skills to gain an unfair advantage is significant. However, ethical conduct dictates that these skills should be employed to foster genuine understanding and collaboration, not to manipulate or exploit others. The goal should be to facilitate open communication and create an environment of trust, not to exploit vulnerabilities. Using this knowledge to gain a competitive advantage at the cost of someone's well-being is a clear breach of ethical principles.

Furthermore, the potential for bias in interpreting nonverbal cues is substantial. Our own preconceived notions, personal experiences, and biases can unconsciously influence our interpretations, leading us to unfairly judge or misinterpret individuals based on stereotypes or prejudices. To counteract this, it's essential to cultivate self-awareness and critical thinking skills. Regular self-reflection on our own biases and assumptions is crucial, ensuring that our interpretations are grounded in objective observation rather than subjective judgment. This includes seeking feedback from others to gain multiple perspectives and challenge our own biases.

Beyond professional contexts, the application of these skills in personal relationships also necessitates ethical considerations. While it can be tempting to analyze loved ones' nonverbal cues to assess their sincerity or emotions, doing so without sensitivity can damage trust and intimacy.

It's crucial to prioritize empathy and respect in personal relationships. Rather than focusing solely on detecting deception, aim to foster open communication and create a safe space for vulnerable expression. Using your observational skills to understand and support loved ones should be done with kindness and empathy, never as a means of controlling or manipulating them.

The ethical use of deception detection knowledge extends to legal and investigative contexts. While law enforcement and investigators may utilize these skills, they must be employed within the framework of the law, ensuring that all actions align with due process and fundamental human rights. The interpretation of nonverbal cues should be used as supporting evidence, not as primary evidence, and should always be weighed against other forms of corroborating evidence. It's vital to avoid jumping to conclusions, and to focus on building a thorough and impartial investigation. False accusations based on misinterpretations can have devastating consequences for the accused.

In conclusion, mastery of deception detection techniques empowers individuals with remarkable abilities, but this power comes with significant ethical responsibilities. The ethical considerations outlined here – respecting privacy, avoiding snap judgments, countering biases, and applying knowledge responsibly in various contexts – are not merely optional; they are essential for the responsible and ethical use of this knowledge. The ability to interpret nonverbal cues should enhance our understanding of human interaction, improve communication, and foster stronger relationships, not be used as a tool for manipulation or exploitation. The ethical application of these skills is crucial for building a more trusting and compassionate world.

The responsible application of deception detection skills requires ongoing learning and self-reflection. Continuously educating oneself on the nuances of nonverbal communication, cultural differences, and potential biases is crucial. Attending workshops, reading relevant literature, and seeking feedback from trusted mentors and peers can enhance one's understanding and improve the accuracy and ethical application of this knowledge. Regular self-assessment is also vital to identify and address personal biases, ensuring that observations are as objective as possible.

Moreover, it's essential to understand the limitations of deception detection. No technique is foolproof; individuals can consciously or unconsciously mask their true feelings, making accurate assessments challenging. Recognizing these limitations fosters humility and prevents overconfidence in one's ability to definitively determine deception. Rather than striving for absolute certainty, the focus should be on gathering information and using it to form informed judgments, always acknowledging the inherent uncertainties in human behavior.

Finally, the ethical application of deception detection skills should be guided by the principle of promoting well-being.
The ultimate goal should be to use this knowledge to improve communication, build trust, and foster healthier relationships, both personally and professionally. Using this knowledge to manipulate or exploit others undermines these principles, resulting in negative consequences for individuals and society. Prioritizing empathy, respect, and fairness in the application of these skills is essential for achieving positive outcomes and upholding ethical standards. By focusing on the responsible application of this knowledge, we can
harness the power of deception detection for the

betterment of ourselves and the world around us. The ethical use of this knowledge is paramount, not merely an addendum to the skillset, but the very foundation upon which it should be built and applied. Only with careful consideration of ethical implications can the powerful tools of deception detection be used for good.

EMPATHY AND CONNECTION THROUGH NONVERBAL UNDERSTANDING

Empathy, at its core, is the ability to understand and share the feelings of another. It's a cornerstone of strong relationships, fostering trust, understanding, and genuine connection. While verbal communication plays a role, nonverbal cues often provide a richer, more nuanced understanding of another person's emotional landscape.

Mastering the art of reading nonverbal communication is therefore crucial for cultivating empathy and building stronger bonds. This involves actively observing not only what someone says, but how they say it, paying close attention to their body language, facial expressions, and tone of voice.

Consider a simple conversation: Someone tells you they're "fine," but their shoulders are slumped, their voice is flat, and they avoid eye contact. The verbal message contradicts the nonverbal signals, strongly suggesting that "fine" is not the accurate reflection of their internal state. By recognizing this incongruence, you can move beyond the surface-level response and inquire further, demonstrating genuine interest and concern. This simple act of observation can significantly deepen the connection, turning a superficial exchange into a meaningful interaction.

The ability to accurately interpret nonverbal cues requires practice and conscious effort. It's not about instantly deciphering every subtle gesture, but rather about developing a keen awareness of the overall communication package. This involves paying attention to clusters of nonverbal cues—multiple signals occurring simultaneously—rather than focusing solely on isolated gestures. For example, a furrowed brow combined with clenched fists and a tense posture strongly suggests anger or frustration, providing a more complete picture than any single element alone.

Furthermore, cultural context plays a crucial role in interpreting nonverbal cues. Gestures that convey one meaning in one culture might have a completely different significance in another. A simple head nod, for example, signifies agreement in many Western cultures, but in some Asian cultures, it can indicate understanding or simply acknowledgement, not necessarily agreement. Therefore, it's essential to be mindful of cultural differences and avoid making assumptions based on your own cultural background. The aim is not to judge or label, but to understand the individual within their own cultural context.

Beyond cultural differences, individual personalities and past experiences also shape nonverbal communication. Someone naturally reserved might have a more subdued body language than someone extroverted, even if they are experiencing the same emotions. Recognizing these individual differences is crucial to avoid misinterpretations.It's also important to remember that]nonverbal communication is not always conscious or deliberate.

Subconscious cues often leak out, offering valuable insight into someone's true feelings and intentions, even if they're trying to hide them.

Developing empathy through nonverbal understanding goes beyond simply observing and interpreting cues. It requires active listening and a genuine desire to understand the other person's perspective. This involves reflecting back what you've observed, checking your understanding with thoughtful questions, and showing genuine compassion. For instance, if you observe someone exhibiting signs of stress or anxiety, you might say, "I noticed you seem a little tense.

Is everything alright?" This demonstrates empathy and creates a safe space for the other person to open up and share their feelings.

In intimate relationships, this empathetic understanding is paramount. It allows partners to navigate conflicts more effectively, understanding each other's needs and concerns. Misunderstandings often stem from misinterpretations of nonverbal cues. By consciously paying attention to each other's body language, tone of voice, and facial expressions, couples can prevent escalation and build a stronger, more trusting bond. Learning to recognize the subtle shifts in mood and emotional state can help anticipate potential conflict and allow for proactive communication.

Similarly, within families, understanding nonverbal cues can significantly improve dynamics. Children, particularly younger ones, often express themselves more through nonverbal communication than verbal language. Parents who are attuned to their children's body language can better understand their needs and emotional state, fostering closer relationships. This same principle applies to sibling relationships, helping siblings better understand each other's emotional reactions and navigate conflicts more constructively.

Beyond personal relationships, the ability to read nonverbal cues is invaluable in navigating social situations. It enhances your social intelligence, enabling you to build rapport more effectively, making a positive first impression, and avoiding social faux pas. By being observant and attuned to the nonverbal signals of those around you, you can better adapt your communication style and create a more positive and comfortable interaction for everyone involved. This is especially important in professional settings, where understanding nonverbal cues can greatly improve communication and collaboration.

In conflict situations, nonverbal communication plays a critical role in de-escalation. Recognizing signs of anger, frustration, or defensiveness in yourself and others allows you to proactively address these emotions before they escalate. Through conscious adjustments in your own body language and tone of voice, you can help create a calmer atmosphere and foster more constructive dialogue. By responding with empathy and understanding, showing through your own nonverbal communication a willingness to listen and collaborate, you create space for a more productive resolution.

Mastering the art of reading people involves more than just detecting deception; it involves cultivating empathy and building stronger relationships. By consciously developing your observational skills, becoming more attuned to nonverbal cues, and practicing active listening, you can deepen your connections with others and foster more meaningful interactions. This is not a skill acquired overnight; it is a journey of continuous learning and self-reflection. With consistent practice, you'll become more attuned to the subtle cues that reveal the emotional landscapes of those around you, ultimately enhancing your ability to connect with others on a deeper level. The power to truly understand is the power to truly connect, creating richer, more rewarding relationships in all aspects of your life. This journey of understanding is a rewarding investment in yourself and the relationships you cherish.

IMPROVING COMMUNICATION IN INTIMATE RELATIONSHIPS

Improving communication in any relationship requires a conscious effort, but in intimate partnerships, where vulnerability and emotional intimacy are paramount, effective communication becomes even more crucial.

Building a strong foundation in a romantic relationship rests heavily on the ability to not only understand your partner's words but also to decipher the unspoken messages conveyed through their body language. The skills honed in previous chapters—observing microexpressions, interpreting posture and gestures, and understanding vocal nuances— are all directly applicable here.

The first step towards improving communication is recognizing that communication itself is not solely a verbal process. Often, the most significant messages are transmitted nonverbally. Consider, for instance, the seemingly innocuous act of your partner sighing. Is it a simple exhalation of breath, or is it laced with frustration or weariness? The context matters immensely. A sigh after a long day at work might indicate fatigue, whereas a sigh during a conversation might signal disagreement or disinterest. Learning to differentiate these subtle nuances requires attentive observation and a willingness to seek clarification.

Equally important is the understanding of mirroring. Mirroring, or the subconscious mimicking of another person's body language, is a powerful indicator of rapport and connection. When we feel comfortable and connected with someone, we often unconsciously adopt similar postures, gestures, and even facial expressions. In an intimate relationship, observing whether mirroring is present (or absent) can offer valuable insights into the current state of the connection. A lack of mirroring might indicate emotional distance or disengagement, signaling a need for greater attention and connection.

Active listening is another fundamental element in improving communication. It's far more than just hearing the words; it involves fully engaging with your partner, paying attention to both their verbal and nonverbal cues. This requires putting aside distractions, maintaining eye contact (without being overly intense), and reflecting back what you've heard to ensure understanding. For example, instead of simply responding to a complaint, try saying something like, "So, what I'm hearing is that you feel frustrated because..." This demonstrates that you're genuinely listening and seeking to understand their perspective.

Beyond active listening, consider the power of touch. Physical touch, when appropriate and consensual, is a powerful form of nonverbal communication. A comforting touch on the arm, a gentle hand squeeze, or a loving embrace can communicate support, empathy, and affection far more eloquently than words. However, it's crucial to be mindful of your partner's personal space and boundaries. What one person finds comforting, another might perceive as intrusive. Observing your partner's reaction to your touch is essential to ensuring it's a positive and connecting experience.

Furthermore, paying attention to the environment can significantly impact communication. A comfortable and relaxed atmosphere fosters open and honest communication. Consider the lighting, temperature, and overall ambiance. A noisy, chaotic environment is rarely conducive to meaningful conversation. Creating a space where both partners feel safe and comfortable is crucial for fostering open dialogue and vulnerability.

Conflicts are inevitable in any relationship, but the way couples navigate disagreements significantly impacts the overall health of the relationship. Understanding how to manage conflict constructively requires a deep understanding of both verbal and nonverbal communication. During disagreements, watch for escalating nonverbal cues like clenched fists, narrowed eyes, or a stiffening posture. These signals can indicate rising tension and the need for a de-escalation strategy. Take a break, calm yourselves, and return to the conversation once emotions have subsided. Remember that the goal is not to "win" the argument but to reach a mutual understanding and resolution.

In addressing conflict, utilize "I" statements to express your feelings and needs without placing blame. For example, instead of saying "You always make me feel ignored," try saying "I feel ignored when..." This shifts the focus from accusing your partner to expressing your own feelings and experience.

Nonverbal cues can also reveal unmet needs or unspoken desires. For instance, if your partner constantly fidgets or avoids eye contact during conversations about the future, it might indicate anxiety or uncertainty about the relationship's direction. These subtle cues often provide insights that verbal communication might not reveal. Approaching these topics with empathy and a willingness to listen openly will foster a more secure and trusting environment.

Learning to interpret your partner's nonverbal cues is an ongoing process. There will be times when you misinterpret signals, and that's perfectly okay. The key is to be open to feedback, apologize when necessary, and continuously strive to understand your partner better. Honest and open communication, coupled with attentiveness to nonverbal cues, will build a strong foundation for a more fulfilling and lasting relationship.

Remember, consistency is key. The skills of observing body language and understanding nonverbal communication are not mastered overnight. It takes consistent effort, practice, and a commitment to self-reflection. The rewards, however, are immeasurable—a deeper understanding of your partner, stronger bonds, and a more fulfilling intimate relationship. By integrating these techniques into your daily interactions, you can cultivate a more empathetic, understanding, and loving partnership, strengthening the connection you share and deepening the emotional intimacy within your relationship.

Consider keeping a journal to document your observations. After conversations with your partner, reflect on their nonverbal cues and how they aligned (or didn't align) with their verbal communication. This practice strengthens your observational skills and aids in self-awareness. You might note, for example, a specific instance where a change in posture or tone accompanied a certain statement, helping you better understand the subtext of their communication.

Furthermore, actively seek feedback from your partner. Explain that you're working on improving your communication skills and ask for their honest input. They might highlight nonverbal cues you're missing or suggest areas for improvement. This open dialogue about communication patterns reinforces the importance of mutual understanding and creates a space for continued growth. This collaborative approach to improving communication fosters a stronger sense of partnership and mutual respect.

Another beneficial practice is to consciously practice mirroring your partner's positive nonverbal cues. If they're exhibiting relaxed posture and a calm demeanor, try subtly mirroring those cues. This encourages a sense of connection and rapport, promoting a more positive and harmonious interaction. However, avoid mirroring negative nonverbal cues, as this might unintentionally reinforce negative emotions.

In conclusion, improving communication in intimate relationships is an ongoing process of learning, understanding, and mutual growth. By applying the techniques discussed—active listening, mindful observation of nonverbal cues, constructive conflict resolution, and a willingness to seek and give feedback—couples can build a stronger, more resilient, and deeply fulfilling partnership.

Remember that communication is a two-way street; it requires both partners' commitment and ongoing effort. The journey of mastering communication is a continuous process of understanding, empathy, and a shared desire to build a strong and lasting relationship based on mutual respect, trust, and genuine connection. The ability to read and interpret nonverbal cues acts as a crucial bridge towards achieving this goal, fostering a deeper, more meaningful bond between partners.

STRENGTHENING FAMILY BONDS THROUGH NONVERBAL AWARENESS

The principles of nonverbal communication, so crucial in romantic relationships, extend equally, if not more profoundly, to the intricate dynamics within families. Family bonds, forged over years of shared experiences, are

susceptible to misunderstandings and conflict, often stemming from a lack of awareness in interpreting unspoken messages. Mastering the art of reading nonverbal cues within the family unit can significantly enhance communication, prevent escalating conflicts, and cultivate a deeper sense of connection and understanding.

Consider the common scenario of a teenager retreating to their room after a seemingly minor disagreement with a parent. The spoken words might have been relatively insignificant, but the accompanying slumped shoulders, averted gaze, and tightened jaw speak volumes about the underlying emotions – hurt, anger, or perhaps even a feeling of being misunderstood. A parent attuned to these nonverbal signals can respond with greater empathy, perhaps offering a sincere apology or initiating a calmer conversation rather than escalating the situation through further reprimand or confrontation. The key lies in recognizing that these nonverbal cues are not necessarily deliberate attempts to manipulate, but rather involuntary expressions of internal states.

Similarly, observing the subtle shifts in body language during family gatherings can offer invaluable insights into the relationships between individual members. A strained smile, fleeting glances away, or a noticeable increase in physical distance between two family members might hint at underlying tension or unresolved conflict. By paying close attention to these nonverbal signals, parents can become more adept at identifying potential problems within the family structure before they escalate into major crises. Early intervention, guided by an understanding of nonverbal communication, can prevent the buildup of resentment and foster a more harmonious environment.

Beyond conflict resolution, nonverbal awareness plays a vital role in building stronger, more positive family interactions. A simple, genuine smile, a warm embrace, or a gentle touch can communicate love, support, and connection far more effectively than any spoken words. These nonverbal cues create a sense of security and belonging, fostering a climate of trust and openness within the family. Children, in particular, are highly receptive to nonverbal cues, often mirroring the emotional state of their caregivers. By consciously employing positive nonverbal communication, parents can cultivate a more positive and supportive family environment.

Consider the power of eye contact. Sustained, loving eye contact between a parent and child communicates affection and attentiveness, strengthening the bond between them.

Conversely, avoiding eye contact may signify disengagement, disinterest, or even disapproval. Understanding these nuances can help parents and children better understand each other's emotional states and strengthen their relationship accordingly.

Furthermore, the ability to accurately interpret nonverbal communication within the family unit can facilitate more effective conflict resolution strategies. When disagreements arise, a conscious effort to observe each family member's body language can provide clues about their emotional state and underlying needs. For example, if one family member exhibits signs of defensiveness (crossed arms, clenched fists, avoiding eye contact), a more empathetic and understanding approach is likely to be more productive than a confrontational one. By acknowledging and validating each family member's feelings, even if you don't necessarily agree with their perspective, you can create a more conducive environment for productive dialogue.

This requires active listening, a skill honed through mindful observation of nonverbal cues. Active listening isn't merely hearing the words being spoken, but also observing the accompanying body language, facial expressions, and tone of voice. It's about fully immersing yourself in the communication process, demonstrating genuine interest and empathy towards the speaker. This can be facilitated through mirroring techniques – subtly mirroring the posture and body language of the speaker to create a sense of rapport and trust.

However, the interpretation of nonverbal cues requires careful consideration and nuance. Cultural differences can significantly influence body language, so what might be considered a sign of disrespect in one culture could be entirely innocuous in another. For example, direct eye contact is often interpreted as a sign of respect and confidence in Western cultures, but in some Eastern cultures, it can be seen as a challenge or sign of disrespect. Therefore, a thorough understanding of cultural contexts is crucial to avoid misinterpretations and potential conflicts.

Furthermore, individual differences also play a significant role. Some individuals may be naturally more expressive than others, while some might exhibit subtle nonverbal cues that require more careful observation. It's crucial to avoid making generalizations based solely on limited observations.

Instead, focus on building a deeper understanding of each individual family member's unique communication style, recognizing that nonverbal cues may vary depending on the context and the individual's personality.

The goal is not to become a mind reader, but rather to become a more perceptive and empathetic communicator.
Improving your ability to observe and interpret nonverbal cues within your family will undoubtedly strengthen bonds and lead to more fulfilling relationships. It's a skill learned through practice, observation, and a genuine desire to understand the people you care about most. Engage in active listening, paying attention to the subtleties of body language, facial expressions, and tone of voice.

Consider specific examples within your own family dynamics. Reflect on past interactions where misunderstandings arose. Can you identify instances where nonverbal cues were misinterpreted or overlooked? What could have been done differently to improve communication and prevent conflict? By critically analyzing past experiences, you can identify patterns and develop strategies for improving future interactions.

For instance, think back to family dinners. Were there noticeable shifts in body language during conversations about specific topics? Did anyone consistently avoid eye contact or exhibit signs of tension or discomfort? Such observations offer valuable insights into underlying dynamics and potential areas of conflict. These insights can guide future conversations, allowing you to approach sensitive topics with greater awareness and empathy.

Similarly, observing children's nonverbal cues during playtime or during homework sessions can provide clues to their emotional states and developmental needs. Recognizing when a child is feeling stressed, frustrated, or overwhelmed through their body language allows you to provide appropriate support and guidance.

The cultivation of nonverbal awareness within the family is an ongoing process, requiring patience, practice, and self-reflection. It's about creating a safe and supportive environment where open communication is encouraged and where each family member feels comfortable expressing their thoughts and feelings, both verbally and nonverbally. By fostering a culture of understanding and empathy, families can build stronger, more resilient, and deeply fulfilling relationships based on mutual respect, trust, and genuine connection.

Building stronger family bonds through nonverbal awareness isn't about manipulating others or deciphering hidden agendas; it's about creating a more harmonious and empathetic environment where each member feels seen, heard, and understood. It's a journey of enhancing emotional intelligence, strengthening relationships, and fostering a deeper sense of connection within the family unit. By embracing the power of observation and understanding nonverbal cues, families can transform their interactions, fostering a more positive, resilient, and ultimately more loving environment for everyone involved. It's an investment in the wellbeing and future of your family.

NAVIGATING SOCIAL SITUATIONS WITH CONFIDENCE

Navigating social gatherings can often feel like navigating a minefield. The unspoken rules, the subtle shifts in energy, the pressure to make a good impression – it's enough to leave even the most confident individuals feeling overwhelmed. But what if I told you that mastering the art of nonverbal communication could dramatically alter your experience, transforming potentially awkward encounters into opportunities for connection and positive interactions?

The key lies in understanding that nonverbal communication isn't just about deciphering lies or hidden agendas. It's about recognizing the subtle cues that reveal a person's emotional state, their level of comfort, and their receptiveness to interaction. By becoming attuned to these cues, you can adjust your own behavior, creating a more harmonious and engaging social dynamic.

Let's start with entering a room. Before you even speak, your body language speaks volumes. A slumped posture, a hurried gait, and a downcast gaze communicate insecurity and disinterest. Conversely, an upright posture, a confident stride, and a warm, open expression project self-assuredness and approachability. Practice walking into a room with intention. Hold your head high, shoulders relaxed, and maintain a pleasant facial expression. This simple act can significantly impact the first impressions you make.

Once you're in the room, the art of making initial connections is crucial. Don't underestimate the power of a genuine smile. A genuine smile engages the muscles around the eyes, creating a crinkle that a forced smile often lacks.

This subtle difference is readily noticeable and communicates authenticity. Combine your smile with open, inviting body language. Keep your arms uncrossed, maintain appropriate eye contact (without staring), and offer a firm handshake if the situation allows. These seemingly small actions collectively convey friendliness and approachability, making others more receptive to engaging with you.

Initiating conversation can be daunting, but remember that the foundation is laid in nonverbal cues. Before you even utter a word, subtly signal your interest through your body language. Turn your body slightly towards the person you wish to approach, creating an opening for engagement. Make eye contact, offer a warm smile, and subtly nod to indicate your attentiveness and interest in what they have to say. This nonverbal invitation makes it much easier to transition into a verbal conversation, minimizing the potential for awkward silences or rejections.

During the conversation itself, active listening is paramount.
Active listening goes beyond simply hearing the words; it involves observing nonverbal cues to fully understand the message being conveyed. Pay attention to their facial expressions, their posture, and their hand gestures. Do their expressions match their words? Is their body language open and relaxed, or tense and closed off? Discrepancies between verbal and nonverbal messages often signal underlying emotions or reservations. By noticing these discrepancies, you can respond with greater empathy and understanding, demonstrating that you're truly engaged in the conversation and valuing their perspective.

Mirroring, a subtle technique often used in negotiations and rapport building, can also be employed in social situations.
Mirroring involves subconsciously replicating the other person's body language, creating a sense of rapport and connection. However, it's crucial to mirror subtly, avoiding overt imitation. The aim is to create a sense of synchrony, not to mimic their every movement. A slight mirroring of posture, hand gestures, or pace of speech can subtly enhance the feeling of connection and understanding, without appearing contrived or manipulative.

Maintaining appropriate personal space is also vital. Respecting personal boundaries demonstrates consideration and awareness, fostering a sense of comfort and ease.

Observe the other person's comfort level and adjust your distance accordingly. If someone seems uncomfortable with close proximity, subtly increase your distance. Conversely, if the conversation is flowing naturally and the other person seems at ease, a slightly closer proximity can enhance the feeling of connection.

Recognizing and responding to subtle cues of disinterest is equally important. If someone repeatedly looks away, avoids eye contact, or crosses their arms, it may indicate a lack of interest or discomfort. Respectfully acknowledging these signals is essential. Don't push the conversation if the other person clearly isn't engaged. Instead, gracefully excuse yourself and move on to other interactions. Respecting someone's boundaries is crucial in maintaining positive relationships.

Leaving a conversation also requires finesse. Don't abruptly disappear. Instead, subtly signal your intention to move on. You can do this by politely excusing yourself to get a drink, to speak with someone else, or to simply take a break. A polite farewell and a warm smile can leave a lasting positive impression.

Beyond individual interactions, understanding group dynamics is also crucial for navigating social situations with confidence. Observe the flow of conversation, the subtle power dynamics within the group, and the unspoken rules of engagement. Entering a group conversation requires tact.
Make eye contact with individuals, subtly signal your intention to join, and wait for a natural pause to speak. Avoid interrupting or dominating the

conversation. Instead,
contribute meaningfully and respectfully, showing an interest in others' perspectives.

Understanding how different cultures influence nonverbal communication is also essential. Gestures that are considered polite in one culture may be offensive in another. Being mindful of cultural differences in personal space, eye contact, and other nonverbal cues is crucial in building bridges and avoiding misunderstandings. Researching common cultural norms before attending social events in unfamiliar settings can prevent awkward situations and foster cross-cultural understanding.

Finally, remember that navigating social situations is a skill that improves with practice. Don't be discouraged by occasional awkwardness or missteps. View each social interaction as an opportunity to learn and refine your skills.

Practice your nonverbal communication in low-stakes settings, and gradually work your way up to more challenging social situations. By consistently observing, adapting, and refining your approach, you'll develop the confidence and finesse to navigate any social situation with greater ease and grace. The art of reading people isn't just about deciphering hidden motives; it's about creating
positive connections and building meaningful relationships. This skill can profoundly impact every facet of your life, from your personal relationships to your professional
success. Mastering nonverbal communication

empowers you to build rapport, navigate complex interactions, and ultimately, live a more fulfilling and connected life.

The confidence gained through understanding these subtle cues is invaluable, transforming social interactions from potential anxieties into opportunities for growth and connection. It is a journey of self-discovery and interpersonal mastery, enriching not just your social interactions, but your overall well-being. The ability to read and respond appropriately to nonverbal cues is an essential life skill. It's a skill that, with dedicated practice and mindful observation, can be honed and perfected, leading to more meaningful connections and a richer, more satisfying social life. Embrace the journey, observe carefully, and practice consistently, and you'll find yourself moving through social situations with a newfound confidence and ease.

CONFLICT RESOLUTION AND NONVERBAL DEESCALATION

Conflict resolution often hinges on more than just the words exchanged; it's deeply intertwined with the unspoken language of nonverbal communication. Misinterpretations of body language can easily escalate a disagreement, while conscious manipulation of these cues can pave the way for a peaceful resolution. Recognizing and responding to nonverbal cues—your own and those of the other person—is crucial for de-escalating tense situations and fostering understanding.

One of the most powerful tools in your conflict resolution arsenal is the ability to mirror the other person's body language subtly. Mirroring, or matching the posture, gestures, and even breathing rate of someone, creates a subconscious sense of rapport and connection. It signals that you're listening attentively and empathizing with their perspective. However, mirroring should be subtle and
natural; overt imitation can come across as

mocking or insincere. Aim for a gentle reflection, not a carbon copy. For example, if the other person leans forward slightly, you might mirror this by gently leaning forward as well. If they slow their speech, you can subtly match the pace of your own responses.

Another key aspect of nonverbal de-escalation is maintaining open and receptive body language. Avoid crossing your arms, which often signals defensiveness or resistance. Keep your shoulders relaxed and your palms visible; this communicates openness and trustworthiness. Maintaining direct eye contact, but without staring intensely, shows that you are engaged and attentive to what the other person is saying. However, be mindful of cultural differences; in some cultures, prolonged eye contact can be interpreted as aggressive or challenging. Adjust your approach based on the individual and cultural context. A gentle, reassuring smile, used appropriately, can also work wonders in de-escalating tension. It conveys understanding and empathy, signaling that you are approachable and willing to listen.
However, a forced or inappropriate smile can have the opposite effect, appearing insincere or dismissive. The key is authenticity.

Vocal tone plays a significant role in nonverbal communication during conflict. A calm, measured tone of voice can dramatically alter the course of a disagreement.
Speaking in a slow, deliberate pace, using a softer volume, and avoiding accusatory language helps to create a less confrontational atmosphere. Conversely, raising your voice or using a sharp,

aggressive tone will almost always exacerbate the situation. Pay attention to your breathing as well. Deep, slow breaths can help you maintain composure and prevent your voice from rising. Consciously controlling your breathing can have a calming effect on both you and the other person. The objective is to create a space for respectful dialogue, where both parties feel heard and understood.

Active listening is not just about hearing words; it's also about observing nonverbal cues. Pay close attention to the other person's body language —their facial expressions, posture, and gestures —to gain a deeper understanding of their emotional state and perspective. Are they fidgeting, indicating nervousness or discomfort? Are their shoulders tense, suggesting stress or anxiety? Are they avoiding eye contact, possibly indicating embarrassment or unwillingness to engage? These cues provide valuable insights that can help you tailor your response and defuse the situation. For instance, if you notice the person is visibly upset, you might offer a comforting gesture like a gentle nod or a reassuring touch (only if appropriate within your relationship).

Recognizing these cues allows for a more empathetic and effective response, fostering understanding and de-escalation.

Spatial awareness is another important factor. Maintaining an appropriate distance, neither too close nor too far, creates a comfortable environment for communication. Standing or sitting too close can feel intrusive and threatening, whereas standing too far away might create a sense of distance and disconnection. Observe the other person's body language to gauge their comfort level with proximity. If they seem uncomfortable or start to back away, give them more space. Conversely, if they lean closer, it may indicate that they feel comfortable and engaged in the conversation. This awareness demonstrates respect for their personal space and helps maintain a positive communication dynamic.

Understanding your own nonverbal cues is just as important as understanding those of the other person. Become aware of your own body language and its impact on the interaction. Are you unconsciously mirroring the other person's negative body language, thus escalating the conflict? Are you exhibiting signs of defensiveness or aggression, such as clenched fists or a rigid posture? Conscious self-awareness allows you to regulate your nonverbal communication and prevent unintended escalation.

Practice makes perfect when it comes to nonverbal communication in conflict resolution. Take opportunities to observe how others handle disagreements, paying attention to their nonverbal cues and the effectiveness of their strategies. Practice consciously controlling your own
nonverbal cues in low-stakes situations, gradually building your confidence and skill in using them to de-escalate tense situations. The ability to navigate conflict effectively is a valuable skill that enhances personal relationships, professional interactions, and overall well-being.

Beyond mirroring, open body language, and controlled vocal tone, consider the power of touch in de-escalation. A gentle touch on the arm or shoulder, if culturally appropriate and acceptable within the relationship, can communicate empathy and reassurance. However, this should be done judiciously, considering the cultural context and the relationship dynamics. An inappropriate touch can worsen the situation. The goal is not to overstep boundaries but to create a sense of connection and understanding through carefully chosen physical cues. Similarly, using silence strategically can be powerful. A thoughtful pause before responding can allow both parties to collect their thoughts and reduce emotional reactivity. It allows for a more measured and rational response.

In addition to these techniques, remember the importance of empathy and understanding. Put yourself in the other person's shoes; try to understand their perspective, even if you don't agree with it. This empathy can be conveyed nonverbally through your facial expressions, posture, and tone of voice. Showing understanding, even without necessarily agreeing, can often go a long way towards de-escalating the situation and fostering a more constructive conversation. Remember that conflict is inevitable in any relationship, but how you manage it can significantly impact its longevity and health.

Furthermore, consider the environment in which the conflict is taking place. A noisy or crowded environment can exacerbate tension. If possible, move to a quieter, more private location where you can both feel more comfortable and focused. The physical setting can significantly impact the tone and outcome of a conversation. A calm, neutral environment, free of distractions, promotes a more conducive atmosphere for resolution. Take a break if the tension becomes overwhelming. Stepping away for a few minutes to collect yourself allows for a calmer approach when you return to the conversation.

The ability to de-escalate conflicts through nonverbal communication is a skill honed over time. It's not about mastering every subtle cue, but about developing a heightened awareness of your own nonverbal cues and those of others, and using this awareness to create a more positive and productive interaction. The ultimate goal is not to win an argument, but to build bridges and foster better understanding, using the power of nonverbal communication as a key tool in that process. Through practice and self-reflection, you will improve your ability to recognize the signs of escalating tension, employ appropriate de-escalation techniques, and ultimately build stronger, healthier relationships. The conscious application of these techniques transforms conflict from a destructive force into an opportunity for growth and understanding. Mastering this crucial aspect of communication is an investment in building stronger, more resilient relationships across all aspects of your life.

ADVANCED MICROEXPRESSION ANALYSIS

Building upon the foundational understanding of microexpressions established in previous chapters, this section explores more nuanced and complex aspects of their analysis. While the earlier chapters provided a basic
framework for recognizing primary emotions like happiness, sadness, anger, fear, surprise, and disgust, this section delves into the complexities of microexpressions that reveal
blended emotions or subtle variations within those primary categories. For instance, a microexpression might momentarily show a flash of contempt masked by a more dominant expression of politeness – understanding this subtle shift requires a higher level of observational skill.

The ability to detect these blended emotions is crucial in many situations. In a negotiation, for example, a person might verbally express agreement while a fleeting microexpression of doubt or concern crosses their face.
Recognizing this subtle incongruence allows for

a more informed approach, potentially leading to a more favorable outcome. Similarly, in a clinical setting, a patient might claim to feel relieved while a brief flash of anxiety betrays their true emotional state. This discrepancy could prompt further exploration and a more effective therapeutic approach.

Advanced microexpression analysis requires not only sharp observation skills but also a deep understanding of human psychology. It necessitates a capacity to integrate multiple nonverbal cues – facial expressions, body posture, hand gestures, and vocal tone – to create a holistic interpretation. A single microexpression, when taken out of context, can be easily misinterpreted. It's the combination of several cues, observed over time, that provides a more accurate understanding of an individual's emotional state.

Consider the example of a person presenting a business proposal. They might express confidence verbally, maintaining steady eye contact and a poised posture.
However, a closer look might reveal subtle microexpressions of anxiety around their mouth or eyes during critical points of their presentation. Combined with fidgeting hands or a slight tremor in their voice, these cues suggest that their outward confidence may be masking underlying apprehension. A skilled observer could use this information to adjust their approach, ensuring the presentation is received more effectively.

To enhance your skills in advanced microexpression analysis, we'll move beyond simply identifying the basic emotions. We'll explore microexpressions representing more nuanced feelings, such as:

Contempt:
This often manifests as a subtle tightening of the mouth, accompanied by a slight raising of one corner of the lip. It's often a quick, almost imperceptible movement, easily missed by the untrained eye. However, its significance lies in revealing disdain or disrespect.

Disgust:
While a classic disgust expression involves wrinkling the nose and upper lip, subtle microexpressions might only involve a slight twitch of the nose or a brief tightening of the lip. These can indicate aversion or revulsion toward a person, idea, or situation.

Fear:
Beyond the well-known wide eyes and open mouth, subtle fear might manifest as a brief widening of the eyes or a slight flinching of the shoulders. These fleeting movements are crucial to detect, as they can signal genuine anxiety or apprehension that a person is consciously trying to conceal.

Sadness:
Subtle sadness might not involve obvious tears or drooping shoulders. A downward turn of the mouth corners, barely noticeable, or a brief clouding of the eyes can hint at underlying sadness or dejection.

Blended Emotions:
Many microexpressions represent a complex blend

of two or more emotions simultaneously. For instance, a person might show a blend of anger and fear, manifesting as a furrowed brow combined with wide eyes and a slight retraction of the lips. This blended expression often reveals a conflicted emotional state.

Developing the ability to identify these complex expressions and blended emotions requires extensive practice and
focused observation. The following exercises will help you refine your skills:

Exercise 1: Slow-Motion Analysis:
Find video footage of individuals engaged in various conversations or presentations. Use a video editing software or player to slow down the footage significantly. This allows you to observe the rapid succession of facial expressions with greater clarity, making it easier to identify microexpressions and analyze their nuances.

Exercise 2: Microexpression Spotting:
Watch short video clips specifically designed to illustrate microexpressions, which are widely available online. Focus on identifying the primary and secondary emotions expressed, paying attention to the subtle variations in muscle movements around the eyes, mouth, and eyebrows. Repeatedly review the videos until you can consistently identify the microexpressions.

Exercise 3: Real-Life Observation:
Observe people in various social settings – coffee shops, meetings, or social gatherings. Practice observing their facial expressions during conversations, focusing on identifying any fleeting

microexpressions. Be mindful of the context and surrounding nonverbal cues to gain a comprehensive understanding.

Exercise 4: Self-Analysis:
Record yourself while discussing a sensitive or emotional topic. Review the recording slowly and carefully, analyzing your own microexpressions. This self-reflection can help you understand how your own emotions might be unintentionally conveyed through subtle facial movements. This improved self-awareness is invaluable for improving your communication skills and emotional intelligence.

Exercise 5: Comparative Analysis:
Compare and contrast multiple microexpressions from different individuals within the same context or experiencing similar emotions. Observe the subtle differences in expression and how these variations might reflect individual personality traits or communication styles.

Mastering advanced microexpression analysis requires patience, persistence, and a commitment to continuous learning. Regular practice using these exercises will
gradually refine your observational skills and deepen your understanding of the subtle nuances of human emotion. The ability to interpret these subtle cues is not just about
detecting deception; it's about developing a deeper understanding of human behavior and building stronger, more authentic relationships. This skill translates to a more profound empathy and the potential for more effective communication across

all aspects of life. With dedication, you can transform your observational abilities from basic awareness to sophisticated interpretation, gaining valuable insights into the unspoken language of human interaction.

ANALYZING BODY LANGUAGE IN SPECIFIC CONTEXTS

Building on our understanding of microexpressions and their subtle variations, let's now explore how these nonverbal cues, coupled with broader body language analysis, manifest in specific contexts. The ability to interpret body language is not a universal skill applicable equally across all situations; instead, the nuances and interpretations shift based on the specific environment and the goals of the individuals involved. Understanding these contextual variations is crucial for accurate interpretation.

Consider, for example, the job interview. Here, the stakes are high. Both the interviewer and the interviewee are actively managing their presentations of self. The interviewer is looking for signs of competence, confidence, and cultural fit; the interviewee is attempting to project these qualities while simultaneously masking nervousness or insecurity. A confident candidate might maintain strong eye contact, sit upright with relaxed but alert posture, and use open hand gestures to emphasize points. Conversely, a nervous candidate may exhibit fidgeting, avoid eye contact, adopt a closed posture with crossed arms or legs, and exhibit nervous tics like touching their hair or face repeatedly.

However, it's crucial to avoid oversimplification. A seemingly confident individual might be masking anxiety through forced displays of confidence—a stiff posture, an overly wide smile that doesn't quite reach the eyes, and infrequent blinking can all be indicators of suppressed nervousness. Similarly, a candidate who appears initially nervous might simply be introverted and needs time to warm up; observing their gradual relaxation and increasing engagement over the course of the interview can reveal a truer picture. The key is to look for patterns and clusters of behaviors rather than relying on single isolated cues.

Presenting to a large audience presents a different set of nonverbal challenges. Here, the focus shifts from individual interaction to audience engagement. Confident presenters typically maintain steady eye contact, scanning the room to connect with individuals rather than focusing on a single point. Their posture is open and expansive, conveying authority and engagement with their material. Gestures are deliberate and purposeful, used to reinforce key points and maintain audience interest. However, these same behaviors can become problematic if overdone. Excessive pacing, overly dramatic hand gestures, or an overly loud voice can detract from the message and appear unnatural, signaling a lack of genuine confidence. Conversely, a presenter who avoids eye contact, displays a slumped posture, or mumbles may appear disengaged and unsure of their material, failing to create the desired impact. The optimal presentation style depends on the audience and context, but in all cases, genuine engagement, combined with clear and confident communication, is key.

Legal settings demand an even higher level of interpretive precision. The stakes are incredibly high, and any misinterpretation can have serious consequences. In courtrooms or during depositions, individuals are often under significant pressure, leading to subtle shifts in body language that can reveal their true feelings and intentions. A witness who avoids eye contact, exhibits inconsistent posture, or provides overly elaborate answers may be attempting to conceal information. Microexpressions, fleeting changes in facial expression that betray suppressed emotions, can be especially valuable in identifying deception.

A fleeting flash of guilt, fear, or anger, even masked by a more dominant expression of calmness, can be a significant indicator. However, it is crucial to remember that body language is not foolproof. Nervousness, cultural differences, or even physical limitations can influence an individual's nonverbal behavior. Therefore, competent interpretation of body language in legal settings requires a profound understanding of the context, and any observations should be corroborative with other evidence, rather than used as the sole basis for judgment. The skill of identifying subtle shifts in behavior under pressure is paramount, requiring an acute awareness of both verbal and nonverbal cues.

The application of body language analysis transcends professional settings, extending to personal relationships as well. In intimate relationships, unspoken communication often speaks volumes. A subtle shift in posture, a fleeting touch, or a change in tone can reveal much more than words alone. Understanding these nuanced cues can foster greater intimacy and empathy, leading to stronger bonds. However, in situations of conflict, heightened emotions can cause these nonverbal cues to become even more complex. A defensive posture, crossed arms, and averted gaze might signal anger or resentment. Similarly, a forced smile that doesn't reach the eyes or overly solicitous behavior could indicate a hidden agenda. It is crucial to remember that understanding body language is not about assigning labels to individuals or making hasty judgments. Instead, it's about developing a more comprehensive understanding of their emotional state and motivations, leading to more constructive communication and resolution of conflicts. The ability to discern genuine from contrived displays of affection or remorse is essential for navigating relationship complexities.

Negotiations represent yet another context demanding astute observation of body language. Successful negotiation involves an understanding of both your own nonverbal cues and those of your counterpart. Maintaining an open, approachable posture, making appropriate eye contact, and using open hand gestures generally signals trustworthiness and cooperation. However, aggressive postures, clenched fists, or interrupting behaviors can escalate tension and damage the negotiation process. The ability to recognize signs of stress, discomfort, or deception in the other party can provide an advantage, allowing you to adjust your strategy accordingly. For instance, a sudden increase in fidgeting, avoidance of eye contact, or frequent throat clearing might suggest that your opponent is uncomfortable with your offer or is concealing important information. Recognizing and responding appropriately to these subtle shifts can be the difference between reaching a mutually beneficial agreement and a failed negotiation. The subtle dance of nonverbal communication within the negotiating table often determines the ultimate outcome.

To further refine your understanding of body language within these various contexts, consider practicing active observation. Watch individuals in different settings, paying close attention to their posture, gestures, facial expressions, and eye movements. Try to identify patterns and clusters of behaviors that may indicate specific emotions or intentions.

Consider recording yourself in different situations and analyzing your own nonverbal cues. This will improve your self-awareness and help you understand how your body language might be interpreted by others. This process of self-reflection and observational practice is essential for developing your skills in reading body language and applying it effectively across a range of situations.

Remember that competence in this field requires continuous learning and refinement; it is a journey, not a destination.

Ultimately, mastering the art of reading people is about developing a keen observation coupled with empathy and context-specific understanding. While body language offers valuable clues, it's not a definitive guide; it's a piece of a much larger puzzle. Combining your understanding of body language with other relevant information, such as verbal communication, environmental cues, and prior knowledge of the individual, allows for a far more accurate and nuanced interpretation. The ability to decipher these nonverbal cues, though challenging, can empower you to navigate complex social and professional situations with greater confidence and effectiveness. It allows for a more empathetic, informed, and ultimately, successful approach to human interaction.

USING TECHNOLOGY TO ENHANCE OBSERVATION SKILLS

Building upon the foundational skills of observing microexpressions and contextualizing body language, we now enter a realm where technology significantly amplifies our observational capabilities. The human eye, while remarkably adept, has limitations in processing speed and detail. Technology, however, offers tools to overcome these limitations, allowing for a more precise and comprehensive analysis of nonverbal communication. This section explores how readily available technologies can transform your ability to interpret subtle cues and deepen your understanding of human behavior.

One of the most impactful applications of technology in observation enhancement is video analysis. Recording interactions, whether professionally or personally, provides a valuable resource for later review. This is particularly useful for situations where immediate analysis is difficult, such as fast-paced conversations or emotionally charged encounters. Consider a business negotiation: the pressure of the moment might obscure subtle shifts in posture or fleeting expressions of doubt from your counterpart. A recording allows you to rewind, pause, and meticulously examine these nonverbal cues at your leisure, identifying patterns and inconsistencies that might have been missed in real-time.

The ability to slow down the footage is particularly significant. Many nonverbal cues, like microexpressions, are incredibly brief—lasting only a fraction of a second. Our brains, often overwhelmed by the continuous flow of information, may not register these fleeting moments.

However, with video analysis software, you can slow the footage down to a near standstill, allowing for a thorough examination of facial muscles, eye movements, and even the slightest shifts in posture. This detailed scrutiny reveals subtle expressions that might otherwise remain hidden, providing significantly more data for your interpretation.

Furthermore, video analysis software often includes frame-by-frame advancement, enhancing the precision of observation. This feature allows for a granular review of each moment, ensuring no nonverbal clue goes unnoticed.

This level of detail is invaluable when analyzing complex interactions, enabling you to pinpoint the exact moment a microexpression occurs, identify its duration, and understand its context within the broader conversation. This is especially helpful in situations requiring detailed assessments, such as forensic investigations or security analysis, where accuracy is paramount.

Beyond simply slowing down footage, advanced video editing software can also enhance the visual clarity.

Adjusting brightness, contrast, and saturation can bring out subtle details, enhancing the visibility of facial nuances that might otherwise be masked by poor lighting or camera quality. Imagine trying to interpret the microexpressions of a suspect during a police interrogation; poor lighting could obscure crucial clues. By enhancing the video's visual quality, the subtle twitch of a muscle or a fleeting widening of the eyes becomes much clearer, allowing for a more accurate interpretation.

The use of technology extends beyond professional contexts. Individuals can utilize these techniques for self-improvement in various social and interpersonal situations. Consider a scenario where you're attempting to understand a friend's emotional state after a challenging event. Instead of relying solely on verbal communication, recording a brief conversation and subsequently analyzing it can provide valuable insights. Slowing down the video allows you to focus on their body language—their posture, hand movements, and facial expressions—offering a more comprehensive understanding of their feelings and concerns. This can lead to more empathetic and effective communication.

While video analysis provides an incredible tool for observational enhancement, ethical considerations are crucial. Always ensure you have the consent of all involved parties before recording and analyzing any video footage. Respect for privacy and the avoidance of misinterpretations are paramount. It's essential to approach this process with sensitivity, awareness, and respect for the individual's rights. Consider the implications of your analysis and avoid making judgments based solely on nonverbal cues, acknowledging that context and other factors play a crucial role.

Another technological tool that complements video analysis is the use of specialized software designed for analyzing facial expressions and body language. These programs often employ sophisticated algorithms to detect microexpressions and other subtle nonverbal cues automatically. While these programs can be a valuable aid, it's crucial to remember that they are tools, not oracles. They should be used to augment human observation, not replace it. The software's output should be critically evaluated and contextualized with your own observations and understanding of the situation.

Furthermore, technology can also enhance our ability to capture and analyze static images. Photographs, for example, offer a snapshot in time that can be examined in detail. High-resolution images allow for a closer inspection of facial features and posture, revealing subtle cues that might be missed in a live interaction or lower-resolution images.

Software tools can magnify specific areas of the image, improving the clarity of minute details, such as the subtle contraction of a muscle around the eyes or a slight tremor in the hands. This detailed scrutiny is especially helpful in situations involving analysis of historical photographs or images from security cameras.

However, relying solely on static images can be misleading. A single photograph lacks the dynamism of a video recording, missing the flow of interaction and the sequence of nonverbal cues. Static images offer a partial picture, useful for specific details but insufficient for a comprehensive understanding of the whole interaction.

Therefore, it's best to use static image analysis in conjunction with video analysis or other observational data, to provide a more robust and contextualized interpretation.

In the digital age, access to a vast amount of information through online resources can significantly improve observational skills. Many websites and online courses offer detailed information on body language, microexpressions, and nonverbal communication. These resources provide valuable learning materials and exercises to hone your skills. By studying various examples and case studies, you gain a deeper understanding of the subtleties of human interaction and the diverse ways in which nonverbal cues manifest themselves across different contexts and cultures. This knowledge greatly enhances the accuracy and efficiency of your own observations.

Moreover, online communities and forums dedicated to body language analysis offer platforms for interaction, feedback, and discussion with other enthusiasts. Sharing observations and interpretations with others can expose you to diverse perspectives and insights, expanding your knowledge base and refining your ability to decipher nonverbal cues.

Constructive criticism and discussion with fellow learners can identify potential biases and blind spots in your observations. Through these online interactions, you can enhance your critical thinking skills and further refine your observation techniques.

In conclusion, integrating technology into your observation practices significantly amplifies your capacity to understand human behavior. From video analysis and slow-motion
replay to specialized software and online resources, technology offers a multitude of tools to enhance your ability to decipher nonverbal cues. However, technology should not replace human judgment and understanding; rather, it acts as a powerful aid, improving accuracy and providing a level of detail that's often beyond the capabilities of the unaided human eye.

Remember always to approach the use of technology ethically and responsibly, respecting the privacy of individuals and using your enhanced skills with sensitivity and empathy. The goal is not to manipulate or deceive, but rather to cultivate a deeper understanding of human interaction and improve your capacity for empathy and authentic connection. This holistic approach —combining technological enhancements with a nuanced, ethical understanding—will transform your observational skills, leading to a more informed and enriched life.

THE ROLE OF NONVERBAL COMMUNICATION IN LEADERSHIP

Building upon our exploration of advanced observation techniques and the technological tools that enhance our ability to read nonverbal cues, we now turn our attention to a critical application: leadership. Effective leadership is not solely about strategic planning and decisive action; it's profoundly influenced by the unspoken language of the body. A leader's nonverbal communication—their posture, gestures, facial expressions, and even their tone of voice—can significantly impact team morale, productivity, and the overall success of their endeavors. Understanding and mastering this aspect of leadership is crucial for inspiring trust, fostering collaboration, and effectively conveying a vision.

The power of nonverbal communication in leadership lies in its capacity to establish immediate rapport and build credibility. Before a single word is spoken, a leader's posture and demeanor convey a sense of confidence, competence, or conversely, insecurity and uncertainty. A slumped posture, averted gaze, or fidgeting hands can undermine even the most eloquently delivered message. Conversely, a leader who stands tall, maintains steady eye contact, and uses open and inviting gestures projects an image of assurance and authority, fostering trust and respect among their team. This initial impression is often critical, forming the foundation upon which subsequent interactions are built.

Consider the impact of a leader's facial expressions. A genuine smile, reflecting warmth and approachability, can create a welcoming environment that encourages open communication and collaboration. Conversely, a perpetually stern or unapproachable expression can create a climate of fear and intimidation, stifling creativity and innovation. The subtle nuances of facial expressions—the microexpressions that momentarily betray underlying emotions—can be particularly revealing, offering insights into a leader's true feelings and intentions. A leader who skillfully manages their facial expressions can project a consistent message of confidence and calm, even when facing challenging situations.

The use of gestures is another crucial element of nonverbal leadership communication. Open and expansive gestures can convey openness, confidence, and a willingness to engage.
Conversely, closed-off or defensive gestures—such as crossed arms or legs—can signal resistance, distrust, or unwillingness to collaborate. The way a leader uses their hands and arms can significantly

influence how their message is received. For instance, a leader who uses purposeful and deliberate gestures can emphasize key points, adding impact and clarity to their communication. However, excessive or distracting gestures can detract from their message, rendering it less effective.

Beyond posture, gestures, and facial expressions, the leader's tone of voice also plays a critical role in effective nonverbal communication. A firm yet gentle tone can create an
atmosphere of calm assurance, particularly useful during stressful situations. Similarly, a measured and articulate pace enhances comprehension and conveys trustworthiness.
Conversely, a harsh or rushed tone can be perceived as aggressive or dismissive, causing subordinates to feel undervalued and unheard. Leaders should be mindful not only of what they say, but how they say it, ensuring that their tone complements and reinforces their verbal message.

Furthermore, the leader's physical proximity to their team members can greatly impact communication effectiveness. A leader who maintains an appropriate distance, neither overly close nor overly distant, conveys respect while fostering a sense of connection. Conversely, invading personal space might be perceived as intimidating or disrespectful, while maintaining excessive distance can feel cold or aloof.
Mastering this aspect of nonverbal communication requires careful observation and sensitivity to individual preferences and cultural norms.

Beyond the immediate impact on team dynamics, nonverbal communication significantly shapes a leader's ability to inspire and motivate. A leader who exhibits confidence, enthusiasm, and passion through their body language will naturally inspire their team to share those same qualities. This contagious energy can significantly boost morale and drive productivity. Conversely, a leader who appears lackluster or unmotivated will likely have a demoralizing effect on their team, leading to decreased productivity and a lack of engagement.

The effective use of nonverbal communication in leadership extends to the art of active listening. Attentive body language—maintaining eye contact, leaning in slightly, nodding occasionally—signals to the speaker that they are being heard and understood. This fosters trust and encourages open communication, creating a more collaborative and productive environment. Conversely, a leader who appears disinterested or distracted, through fidgeting or avoiding eye contact, conveys a lack of respect and can undermine the speaker's confidence.

The importance of congruence between verbal and nonverbal communication cannot be overstated. A leader who says one thing but communicates something entirely different through their body language will inevitably erode trust and credibility. Incongruence between verbal and nonverbal messages is often the first sign of deception or manipulation, creating an atmosphere of suspicion and distrust within the team. Leaders should strive for congruence, ensuring that their nonverbal cues reinforce and support their verbal message, projecting honesty, integrity, and authenticity.

Consider the scenario of a leader delivering difficult news to their team. While the verbal message might focus on restructuring and potential job losses, the leader's nonverbal cues – a furrowed brow, averted gaze, or a hesitant tone – can significantly amplify the negative impact of the announcement. Conversely, a leader who approaches the same situation with confident posture, empathetic facial expressions, and a reassuring tone can mitigate the anxiety and apprehension of their team, easing the transition and fostering collaboration. This demonstrates how powerful nonverbal communication is in shaping a team's response to even the most challenging circumstances.

The use of nonverbal communication in leadership also extends to the crucial arena of negotiation and conflict resolution. A confident and assertive posture, coupled with open and inviting gestures, can establish a position of
strength during negotiations without appearing aggressive or confrontational. Similarly, empathetic facial expressions and a calm, reassuring tone can help to de-escalate tense situations and foster a more collaborative approach to conflict resolution. By mastering the art of nonverbal communication, leaders can significantly improve their effectiveness in negotiating favorable outcomes and resolving conflicts constructively.

Moreover, cultural considerations are paramount

when interpreting and using nonverbal communication in leadership roles. Gestures, expressions, and proxemics (personal space) vary considerably across different cultures.

A gesture that might convey one meaning in one culture could be interpreted entirely differently in another. A leader who is sensitive to these cultural nuances will be able to communicate effectively across diverse teams and avoid unintended misunderstandings. This cross-cultural awareness is vital in fostering inclusivity and building strong, cohesive teams in today's increasingly globalized world.

Finally, continuous self-awareness and mindful practice are crucial for developing effective nonverbal communication skills in leadership. Leaders should regularly practice self-reflection, paying close attention to their own body language and its potential impact on others. Seeking feedback from trusted colleagues or mentors can also provide valuable insights into areas for improvement. By consciously honing their nonverbal communication skills, leaders can significantly enhance their effectiveness and build stronger, more successful teams. The art of reading and using nonverbal communication is a continuous process of learning, observation, and refinement, essential for leaders who want to truly inspire and influence others. By mastering this crucial aspect of communication, leaders can cultivate strong relationships, motivate their teams to achieve extraordinary results, and ultimately build a more effective and successful organization.

INTEGRATING OBSERVATION AND ANALYSIS

Developing a keen intuition isn't about possessing some mystical sixth sense; it's about cultivating a powerful synergy between meticulous observation and insightful analysis. It's a skill honed through practice and self-

awareness, transforming raw data – the subtle shifts in posture, the fleeting expressions, the barely perceptible hesitations – into a comprehensive understanding of the individual before you. This process starts with sharpening your observational skills. We've already explored the intricacies of body language, microexpressions, and vocal cues. Now, let's move beyond simply identifying these individual elements and learn to weave them together into a cohesive narrative.

Consider this: you're in a negotiation. The other party maintains steady eye contact, a seemingly positive sign.

However, their hands are clasped tightly in their lap, a gesture often indicative of tension or anxiety. Their voice, while even-toned, lacks the usual inflection and enthusiasm. Taken individually, each of these cues might offer a partial picture. But by integrating these observations, a more complete and nuanced understanding emerges. The steady eye contact might be a deliberate attempt to project confidence, masking underlying nervousness revealed by the clenched hands and subdued voice. This integrated analysis gives you a far more accurate read of the situation and allows you to adapt your approach accordingly.

This holistic approach requires more than just passive observation. It demands active listening – not merely hearing the words spoken, but paying attention to the *way* they are spoken. Is the voice hesitant, forceful, or measured? Do pauses punctuate the conversation in significant ways? Are there any noticeable discrepancies between the verbal message and the nonverbal cues? These inconsistencies often point to underlying deception or emotional turmoil. For instance, someone vehemently denying involvement in an incident might subtly touch their nose, a common unconscious gesture associated with deception. Combined with a shifting gaze and a rapid change in breathing, this paints a clearer picture than the verbal denial alone.

To further enhance your intuitive abilities, cultivate the practice of contextual awareness. Understanding the setting, the individuals involved, and their relationship dynamics is crucial. A slight frown might indicate annoyance in a formal business meeting, but could simply be a sign of concentration during a game of chess. A nervous laugh in a job interview might betray insecurity, but could stem from a genuine attempt to alleviate tension in a high-stakes situation. By considering the context, you can avoid misinterpretations and develop more accurate assessments.

Moreover, practice mindful observation. This means slowing down, resisting the urge to jump to conclusions, and allowing yourself to fully absorb the information presented before you. Avoid making snap judgments based on limited data. Instead, gather multiple data points over time, carefully noting patterns and inconsistencies. Remember, individuals are complex, and their behavior is rarely monolithic. A single gesture or expression is rarely definitive. It's the accumulation of evidence, the patterns that emerge over time, that allows for a more accurate and insightful understanding.

Developing your intuition also involves cultivating your analytical skills. This is where your knowledge of psychology, body language, and human behavior comes into play. The more you know about these fields, the more effectively you can interpret the nonverbal cues you observe. Use your knowledge of microexpressions to detect fleeting emotional shifts, recognize the subtle signs of deception, and understand the underlying motivations driving behavior.

Beyond the theoretical understanding, practice active analysis. This includes actively questioning your initial assumptions, considering alternative explanations, and continuously refining your interpretations based on new information. Don't be afraid to admit when you're unsure, and always strive for intellectual humility. The goal is not to be infallible, but to constantly improve your ability to read people accurately and intuitively.

This process also entails engaging in deliberate practice.
This isn't about passively observing people; it's about actively engaging in exercises designed to enhance your observational and analytical skills. Practice observing individuals in diverse settings – a bustling marketplace, a quiet library, a formal dinner party. Pay attention to their body language, their tone of voice, their facial expressions, and the way they interact with their environment.
Afterwards, reflect on your observations. What patterns did you notice? What conclusions did you draw? Were your conclusions accurate? What could you have done
differently? This process of self-reflection is critical for continuous improvement.

Furthermore, utilize technological tools to enhance your observational capabilities. While technology shouldn't replace careful observation, it can complement it. Tools such as video recording and slow-motion playback allow for more detailed analysis of microexpressions and subtle body language cues that might otherwise be missed. These
technological aids provide a valuable means of learning and refining your observational skills. However, remember that technology is simply a tool; the true art lies in the interpretation and

integration of the information gathered.

Develop a habit of recording and analyzing your observations. Keep a journal to document the nonverbal cues you notice in different social interactions. Note the context, the individual's behavior, your interpretation, and any subsequent developments that might confirm or contradict your initial analysis. This methodical approach transforms your observations into a valuable learning resource, enhancing your ability to identify patterns and refine your intuition.

Beyond the practical exercises, embrace continuous learning.
Stay updated on the latest research in psychology, body language, and nonverbal communication. Read books, attend workshops, and explore online resources to broaden your knowledge and refine your skills. The more you know, the more effective your intuitive abilities will become.
Remember that intuition isn't a static skill; it's a dynamic process of continuous learning and refinement.

Finally, remember the importance of ethical considerations. The ability to read people accurately is a powerful tool, and it's crucial to use it responsibly and ethically. Avoid using your skills to manipulate or deceive others. Instead, focus on using your abilities to build stronger relationships, foster empathy, and make more informed decisions in your personal and professional life. Ethical application is paramount in leveraging the power of intuitive understanding. This nuanced understanding, cultivated through observation, analysis, and ethical consideration, allows you to navigate complex social situations with greater confidence and build genuinely meaningful connections. It transforms you from a passive observer into an active and insightful participant in the rich tapestry of human interaction.

APPLYING THE SKILLS LEARNED

This chapter delves into real-world scenarios, showcasing the practical application of the nonverbal communication skills developed throughout the book. We'll examine diverse situations, highlighting how subtle cues, when interpreted correctly, can provide valuable insights into others' thoughts, intentions, and emotional states. These case studies are designed to solidify your understanding and demonstrate the versatility of the techniques you've learned.

Let's begin with a case study in the realm of professional negotiations. Imagine you're a seasoned salesperson presenting a lucrative proposal to a potential client. The client, initially appearing engaged, begins exhibiting subtle shifts in their body language. Their arms, which were initially open and relaxed, now cross defensively across their chest. Their gaze, previously steady and focused, now darts around the room, avoiding direct eye contact. Their facial expressions, while not overtly negative, reveal fleeting microexpressions of doubt or concern, such as a quick tightening of the lips or a slight furrow of the brow. While verbally expressing interest, their nonverbal cues suggest a level of discomfort or hesitancy.

A skilled observer would recognize this incongruence between verbal and nonverbal communication. Instead of pressing forward with the sales pitch, a wiser approach would involve acknowledging the client's unspoken

concerns. A question like, "I notice you seem to have some reservations. Is there anything specific about the proposal that's causing you to hesitate?" would open the door for further discussion, allowing you to address underlying objections and potentially salvage the deal. Ignoring these nonverbal cues could lead to a lost opportunity, underscoring the importance of attentive observation in high-stakes situations. The successful outcome hinges not just on presenting a strong proposition, but also on interpreting and responding effectively to the subtle signals the client is sending. This case emphasizes the value of observing clusters of nonverbal cues – the combined effect of crossed arms, averted gaze, and microexpressions – rather than focusing on individual signals in isolation.

Now, let's consider a scenario from the personal realm. A couple is experiencing persistent conflict in their relationship. During a tense conversation, one partner repeatedly avoids eye contact, their shoulders slumping, indicating low confidence or a lack of willingness to engage. Their voice tone is flat and monotone, even when expressing supposed affection, revealing a lack of congruency between their words and their emotional state. The other partner, while attempting to resolve the issue, fails to recognize these crucial cues, focusing solely on the verbal content of the conversation. This leads to misunderstandings, exacerbating the conflict instead of resolving it.

In this instance, understanding the nonverbal signals would be critical. The avoidance of eye contact and the slumped posture signal discomfort and emotional withdrawal. The monotone voice reveals a lack of genuine investment in the conversation. Recognizing these nonverbal indicators allows the other partner to approach the situation with greater empathy and sensitivity. Instead of directly confronting the partner, a more effective approach might involve creating a more comfortable environment, encouraging open communication through active listening, and addressing the underlying emotional issues revealed by the nonverbal cues. By actively seeking to understand the unspoken message, the couple can pave the way for constructive dialogue and relationship improvement. This highlights the power of nonverbal awareness in fostering healthier relationships.

Another example involves a job interview. The candidate, while articulating impressive qualifications and experiences, exhibits fidgeting behavior such as repeatedly adjusting their clothing or tapping their foot. Their hands frequently touch their face, and their gaze darts nervously around the room, avoiding consistent eye contact with the interviewer. Despite the impressive resume, these nonverbal cues suggest nervousness, anxiety, or a potential lack of confidence.

While these actions may stem from simple nervousness, a savvy interviewer should take note. These are cues that might indicate difficulties with handling pressure or working independently. The interviewer might address this, demonstrating empathy by mentioning the stressful nature of the interview and exploring the candidate's strengths through more open-ended questions that might ease their

nervousness. Again, this shows how interpreting nonverbal cues alongside verbal information provides a more complete and reliable assessment.

Let's shift to a slightly different scenario, focusing on parental interactions. A parent is attempting to discipline a child who has misbehaved. The child's body language speaks volumes. Their shoulders are hunched, arms are pulled close, and they avoid eye contact. While the child may be verbally defiant or argumentative, these nonverbal cues clearly

indicate fear or apprehension. A parent, understanding these signals, can adapt their disciplinary approach. Instead of resorting to further reprimand, a kinder, more empathetic approach might involve creating a sense of safety and understanding, allowing the child to express their feelings without feeling threatened. This illustrates the importance of nonverbal communication in parenting, helping foster healthy relationships between parents and children.

Consider a scenario in a courtroom setting. A witness is giving testimony, verbally maintaining innocence, yet displaying subtle inconsistencies in their body language. They frequently touch their nose, a gesture often associated with deception, and their gaze avoids contact with the jury and the prosecution. Their voice tone shifts, sometimes higher and faster when discussing certain details, further highlighting nervousness and potential deception. A skilled lawyer, adept at reading nonverbal communication, would take note of these inconsistencies, utilizing them to subtly challenge the witness's testimony, leading to a more thorough examination of the facts.

Let's look at the everyday scenario of making friends. You meet someone new at a party. They constantly check their watch, avoid prolonged eye contact, and their body faces away from you slightly. Their responses to your questions are short and lack enthusiasm. While they may verbally express interest in continuing the conversation, their nonverbal cues clearly indicate a disinterest in connecting. Respecting these nonverbal clues and moving on to interact with others shows social intelligence and an understanding of nonverbal cues.

Finally, consider a case in customer service. A customer enters a store appearing frustrated. They speak curtly, their brow is furrowed, and their arms are crossed tightly across their chest. While stating their issue, their voice is tight and their body tense. A skilled service professional will not only focus on resolving the problem at hand but will acknowledge the customer's frustration through empathy and attentiveness to their nonverbal cues. A simple acknowledgement such as "I see you seem upset, let me see what I can do to help you" goes a long way toward de-escalating the situation.

These real-world examples highlight the critical role of nonverbal communication in various contexts. By mastering the art of observation, integrating verbal and nonverbal cues, and understanding cultural nuances, you can significantly enhance your ability to build stronger relationships, navigate complex situations, and develop a deeper understanding of human behavior. The ability to read people effectively is not about deception detection alone; it's about cultivating

empathy, improving communication, and building more meaningful connections. The key is to continually practice your observational skills, refine your ability to interpret nonverbal cues, and remember that context is key to accurate interpretation. With consistent effort and practice, you will become increasingly adept at understanding the unspoken messages that surround us daily.

DEVELOPING YOUR PERSONAL STRATEGY FOR READING PEOPLE

Developing a robust personal strategy for reading people isn't about adopting a rigid, one-size-fits-all approach. It's about understanding the core principles and adapting them to your specific needs and goals. Think of it as crafting a tailored suit—the fabric is the foundational knowledge you've gained thus far, but the cut, style, and fit must be personalized to you. This personalization begins with honest self-reflection.

What are your primary goals for improving your ability to read people? Are you hoping to enhance your professional relationships, improve your personal connections, or perhaps navigate challenging social situations with more confidence?

Identifying your goals will determine the specific areas of nonverbal communication you should prioritize. For example, if your goal is to improve business negotiations, you'll need to focus on detecting signs of deception, assessing power dynamics through posture and eye contact, and interpreting subtle shifts in mood that might signal a change in the other party's stance. If your goal is to build stronger personal relationships, you'll want to hone your skills in empathy, picking up on the emotional cues of loved ones, and understanding their nonverbal expressions of affection, frustration, or sadness.

Once you've identified your goals, consider your personal strengths and weaknesses. Are you naturally observant, or do you need to develop your attention to detail? Are you quick to judge, or do you tend to approach interactions with an open mind? Recognizing your predispositions is crucial to developing an effective strategy. If you're already highly observant, you might focus on refining your interpretive skills, learning to distinguish between genuine and feigned emotions. If you tend to jump to conclusions, you might concentrate on practicing mindful observation, slowing down your initial judgments, and gathering more data before drawing conclusions.

Creating a personalized checklist can be invaluable. This checklist doesn't need to be exhaustive, but it should highlight the key nonverbal cues you'll be looking for based on your goals and your preferred communication style. For instance, your checklist might include:

Facial expressions:
Specifically, what subtle microexpressions (brief, involuntary facial movements) should you be watching for? Are you particularly interested in detecting signs of deception, such as lip compression or fleeting glances to the side? Or are you more focused on

identifying genuine emotions like joy, sadness, or anger?

Your checklist should include the specific expressions relevant to your goals.

Body language:

What postures or gestures are particularly relevant in your context? Are you trying to discern dominance or submission in a negotiation? Or are you trying to understand someone's level of comfort or engagement in a social situation? Your checklist might include specific body language indicators like open or closed posture, crossed arms, fidgeting, mirroring behavior, or lack of eye contact.

Eye contact:

Is consistent eye contact important in your context, or does a lack of it suggest something else entirely? The cultural context is paramount here. Consider the cultural norms of the individuals you interact with most often, as these greatly influence the interpretation of eye contact.

Does avoiding eye contact signal shyness, deceit, or simply cultural politeness?

Voice tone and pace:

Vocal cues can be incredibly revealing. Does a high-pitched voice indicate nervousness?

A slower pace of speech suggest careful consideration or deception? Paying attention to paralinguistic cues (nonverbal aspects of speech) can often provide crucial context to the verbal message.

Beyond creating a checklist, you need to develop a

strategy for actively practicing your observational skills. Don't just passively observe; actively engage in situations where you can test your newly acquired skills. Start with low-stakes interactions, such as observing people at a coffee shop or a park. Focus on identifying nonverbal cues and practice formulating hypotheses based on your observations. Then, compare your hypotheses to the actual behavior of the individuals. Gradually increase the complexity of the scenarios, engaging in conversations that allow you to put your skills to the test.

Reflect on your experiences. Maintain a journal to document your observations, hypotheses, and outcomes. Analyze what you got right, and more importantly, what you got wrong.

Honest self-reflection is key to continuous improvement.
Were your initial interpretations accurate? What factors influenced your perceptions, and what could you have done differently? By consistently reviewing your observations and adjusting your strategy accordingly, you will gradually enhance your ability to read people effectively.

Furthermore, cultivate self-awareness. Your own nonverbal communication significantly impacts how others respond to you. If you project confidence and openness, people will be more likely to be open and receptive towards you.

Conversely, if you exhibit anxiety or defensiveness, you may inadvertently create barriers to effective communication. Practicing mindful self-regulation – being aware of your own body language and adjusting it appropriately – will enhance your ability to establish rapport and encourage openness in others.

Finally, remember the importance of context. A single nonverbal cue rarely tells the whole story. Consider the situation, the relationship between the individuals involved, and the cultural norms at play before drawing conclusions. A clenched jaw, for instance, might indicate anger in one context but concentration or determination in another.

Always strive for holistic interpretations, considering multiple cues in conjunction with the surrounding circumstances.

Develop a system for integrating your observations into your decision-making process. Don't let your observations become mere speculation; use them to inform your actions and interactions. If you observe signs of discomfort or disengagement in a negotiation, adapt your approach accordingly. If you perceive signs of deception, delve deeper, asking clarifying questions or seeking further confirmation. Your ability to accurately read people shouldn't be a tool for manipulation but a resource for building stronger relationships, resolving conflict effectively, and making better decisions.

Remember, developing your personal strategy for reading people is an ongoing process, not a destination. Consistent practice, self-reflection, and a willingness to adapt your approach will gradually enhance your skills and empower you to navigate human interactions with greater confidence and understanding. The more you practice, the more intuitive your skills will become, transforming the art of reading people from a conscious effort into a natural ability. The journey of mastering the art of reading people is continuous and rewarding; it's about refining your perception, expanding your understanding, and building more meaningful connections. Embrace the process of continuous learning and refinement, and you'll find your skill in reading people to be an invaluable asset throughout your life. The ultimate goal isn't to become a mind reader but to become a more perceptive and empathetic communicator.

MAINTAINING ETHICAL STANDARDS AND AVOIDING MISINTERPRETATIONS

The power to discern unspoken emotions and intentions, to decipher the subtle language of the body, is a potent tool. Mastering the art of reading people, as explored throughout this book, unlocks a deeper understanding of human interaction, enriching personal and professional relationships. However, this newfound ability carries with it a significant ethical responsibility. It's not enough to simply learn the techniques; we must also grapple with the moral implications and potential for misuse. This section serves as a crucial reminder of the ethical considerations involved, emphasizing the respectful and responsible application of the knowledge you've gained.

One of the most significant ethical concerns centers around the potential for manipulation. The ability to interpret subtle nonverbal cues can be used to influence others, to subtly guide their thoughts and actions. This manipulation could range from subtle persuasion in a sales context

to more ethically questionable tactics designed to exploit
vulnerabilities. Consider, for example, the implications of using knowledge of microexpressions to exploit a person's emotional state during a negotiation. Recognizing a fleeting moment of doubt or uncertainty could be used to leverage a more favorable outcome, but such an approach undermines the principles of fair and equitable interaction. Ethical practice demands that we use our skills for good, not for personal gain at the expense of others.

Respect for individual autonomy is paramount. Each person has the right to privacy and self-expression, free from unwarranted scrutiny or judgment. While observation is an essential component of reading people, it must be conducted with sensitivity and respect. Staring intently at someone, for instance, can be perceived as intrusive and threatening, even if your intentions are purely observational. Maintaining a respectful distance, both physically and emotionally, is crucial. It's about subtly observing, not aggressively scrutinizing. Our goal isn't to dominate or control the interaction, but rather to better understand and connect with others.

The information gleaned through observing nonverbal cues should never be used to label or categorize individuals. Reducing someone to a simple interpretation of their body language ignores the complexity of human experience. Every person is a unique blend of experiences, motivations, and cultural backgrounds, making generalizations about character based on isolated observations inherently flawed and potentially harmful. Avoid the temptation to jump to conclusions based on a single gesture or facial expression. Instead, strive to understand the context of the behavior and the individual's overall presentation. Context is critical. A tense posture, for instance, could be due to stress, anxiety, or simply discomfort in the surroundings. Without understanding the context, any interpretation risks being completely inaccurate.

Another crucial ethical aspect is the accurate and responsible interpretation of data. Body language is incredibly nuanced and context-dependent. A single gesture, taken out of
context, can be completely misinterpreted. For example, crossed arms can be a sign of defensiveness, but it could also simply be a comfortable posture or a response to cold
temperatures. Similarly, a lack of eye contact might indicate deceit, but it could also stem from shyness, cultural norms, or neurological conditions. To avoid misinterpretations, always consider the entire picture. Corroborate your observations with other verbal and nonverbal cues, and remember that your interpretations are never absolute truths, only educated estimations.

Furthermore, it's essential to be mindful of the potential for cultural biases to influence our interpretations. Nonverbal communication varies significantly across cultures. Gestures that are considered polite or neutral in one culture might be offensive or disrespectful in another. For example, a thumbs-up gesture, considered positive in many Western cultures, can be an insult in certain parts of the Middle East.

Therefore, cultural sensitivity is crucial to avoid misinterpretations and offensive generalizations. Educating yourself about different cultural norms and practices is a necessary step in responsible observation.

Furthermore, the knowledge gained should never be used to reinforce existing prejudices or stereotypes. The ability to read people should not be weaponized against marginalized or vulnerable groups. Instead, it should be used to promote understanding, empathy, and inclusivity. Our goal should be to bridge divides, not create them. This responsibility
extends to all contexts – personal, professional, and social. Understanding body language should never come at the cost of ethical considerations.

Transparency and honesty are vital. While it may not always be appropriate to explicitly state that you are analyzing someone's body language, it's generally advisable to be transparent in how you interact with people. This could mean simply being more aware of your own nonverbal cues and how they might be perceived by others. This ensures that interactions are open, honest, and respectful.

Finally, continuous self-reflection is crucial. Regularly examine your own biases and assumptions, challenging your

 own interpretations and seeking feedback from trusted sources. This ongoing process of self-assessment will help to ensure that you remain ethically responsible in your use of these skills. It's a lifelong commitment to self-improvement and responsible application. Regularly reviewing and reevaluating your approach to reading people is necessary to prevent misinterpretations and ensure ethical conduct.

The ability to read people is a powerful skill, but with great power comes great responsibility. The ethical considerations outlined here aren't merely suggestions; they are essential guidelines for the responsible and beneficial application of this knowledge. By incorporating these principles into your practice, you can leverage your understanding of human behavior to build stronger, more authentic relationships, while upholding the highest ethical standards. Remember that the goal isn't manipulation or control, but understanding, empathy, and connection. Using this skill responsibly enhances human connection rather than exploits it. It's about building bridges, not walls; fostering empathy, not judgment. The ethical use of this knowledge is paramount to ensuring positive outcomes in all your interactions. The journey to mastering the art of reading people is a continuous process of learning, refining, and self-reflection. By prioritizing ethical considerations, you not only protect others but also cultivate a deeper understanding of your own capabilities and limitations, strengthening your skillset and ensuring its positive application throughout your life. The ultimate
reward lies in the creation of more meaningful and ethical connections.

RESOURCES AND FURTHER EXPLORATION

The journey towards mastering the art of reading people doesn't end with the closing of this book. It's a continuous process of refinement, learning, and adaptation, much like the ever-evolving nature of human interaction itself. To truly deepen your understanding and hone your skills, continued learning and exploration are essential. This section serves as a gateway to further resources, guiding you towards a richer understanding of nonverbal communication and its practical applications.

One of the most valuable tools in your arsenal will be continued engagement with reputable sources dedicated to the study of body language and nonverbal communication.

Numerous books delve far deeper into specific areas, offering detailed analyses and practical exercises to refine your observation skills. Seek out works focusing on microexpressions, the subtle and fleeting facial movements that often reveal concealed emotions. These texts can provide detailed descriptions, accompanied by images or videos, to aid in your identification of these critical cues.

Consider researching books dedicated to specific cultural nuances in nonverbal communication, as these vary significantly across different societies. A deeper understanding of these differences is vital for accurate interpretation and avoids misinterpretations stemming from cultural misunderstandings. Pay close attention to authors with strong academic backgrounds in psychology, sociology, or related fields, ensuring the information provided is grounded in rigorous research and avoids the pitfalls of pseudoscience.

Beyond books, the internet offers a treasure trove of information. A quick search will yield a wealth of websites, blogs, and online articles dedicated to body language and nonverbal communication. However, it is crucial to approach these sources with a critical eye. Not all information online is accurate or reliable. Look for websites associated with reputable universities, research institutions, or experienced professionals in the field. Be wary of sites promoting quick fixes or unrealistic promises. Quality information will be grounded in research and provide a balanced perspective, acknowledging the complexities and nuances of human behavior. Consider joining online forums or communities focused on body language analysis. These platforms provide opportunities for discussion, sharing experiences, and
learning from others' insights. Remember that engaging in thoughtful discourse with like-minded individuals can significantly enhance your learning process.

Online courses and workshops represent another excellent avenue for continued learning. Many reputable institutions offer courses on nonverbal communication, covering topics such as microexpressions, deception detection, and interpersonal dynamics. These courses often include interactive exercises, real-world case studies, and feedback from experienced instructors, providing valuable

opportunities to apply what you've learned and receive personalized guidance. When choosing an online course, look for those with structured curricula, experienced

instructors, and positive student reviews. Consider factors such as the course length, the level of interaction with the instructor and fellow students, and the availability of

supplementary materials. A well-structured online course will provide a solid framework for enhancing your understanding and skills in a focused and systematic manner.

Beyond formal learning environments, actively engaging in observation exercises can significantly enhance your skills.

Dedicate time each day to observing people in various settings, focusing on their nonverbal cues. Pay attention to their posture, facial expressions, hand gestures, and eye movements. Try to interpret their unspoken emotions and intentions, based on the knowledge you have gained. Begin with simple observations, such as interpreting basic

emotions like happiness or sadness. Gradually increase the complexity of your observations, attempting to detect more subtle cues and hidden emotions. Record your observations and later reflect on your interpretations. This process of active observation and self-reflection is essential for refining your skills and identifying areas for improvement.

Remember, observing people should always be done ethically and respectfully. Avoid staring or making people feel uncomfortable. Your aim is to understand, not to judge or manipulate. Respect people's privacy and boundaries, ensuring your observations are conducted in a non-invasive manner. The ethical implications of this knowledge should always guide your practice.

As you continue your learning journey, don't hesitate to seek out mentorship from experienced professionals in the field. Networking with individuals experienced in body language analysis, communication, or related fields can provide valuable guidance, feedback, and support. These mentors can offer insights into practical applications, share their experiences, and help you navigate potential challenges.

Attend conferences, workshops, or seminars related to nonverbal communication to network with peers and expand your professional network. Engaging with experienced professionals can offer invaluable opportunities for learning and personal growth.

Furthermore, consider exploring related fields to expand your understanding. A solid grasp of psychology, particularly social psychology, will provide a deeper understanding of the underlying motivations and emotions driving human behavior. Similarly, studying communication theories will enhance your ability to analyze and interpret verbal and nonverbal messages within their contextual

framework. Knowledge of criminology or investigative techniques can enhance your ability to detect deception and analyze situations requiring detailed observation and analysis. Exploring these interconnected disciplines provides a richer and more nuanced understanding of human interaction.

The study of microexpressions, in particular, warrants dedicated attention. These fleeting facial expressions, lasting only fractions of a second, often reveal concealed emotions.

Dedicated study, often involving specialized training and practice, is necessary for reliable detection. Seek out resources focusing on microexpression analysis, and consider practicing with video recordings to enhance your recognition skills. Accurate interpretation requires meticulous attention to detail and a deep understanding of facial anatomy and muscle movements. Remember that proficiency in microexpression analysis comes with dedicated practice and refinement.

Case studies can offer invaluable practical application of the knowledge you've gained. Analyze real-life scenarios, such as interviews, negotiations, or social interactions, focusing on the interplay between verbal and nonverbal cues. Reflect on your observations, identify potential biases, and refine your interpretations. This active engagement with real-world examples will solidify your understanding and improve your ability to analyze complex social situations. Use the ethical considerations discussed earlier as a guide, ensuring your analysis prioritizes empathy and respectful understanding.

Finally, remember that your learning journey is a personal one. Adapt your approach based on your own strengths and weaknesses, and don't be afraid to experiment with different techniques and resources. Engage with the material in a manner that resonates with your learning style, utilizing diverse learning tools and resources. Consistent practice, self-reflection, and a dedication to ethical application are key to mastering this valuable skill. The rewards of understanding human behavior are immense, leading to enriched relationships, improved communication, and a deeper understanding of the world around you. The journey to becoming a master of reading people is an ongoing process of learning, refinement, and self-discovery. Embrace this journey, and let it enrich your life in ways you never imagined.

EXERCISES AND CHALLENGES

Now that we've explored the theoretical underpinnings of reading people—from understanding microexpressions to deciphering posture and gestures—it's time to put your newfound skills into practice. This section provides a series of exercises and challenges designed to solidify your understanding and build your confidence in interpreting nonverbal cues. Remember, the key to mastery lies not just in knowledge, but in application. The more you practice, the sharper your observational skills will become, and the more intuitive your understanding of human behavior will be.

Let's begin with some fundamental exercises focusing on individual nonverbal cues. First, gather a collection of short video clips showcasing various emotional states—happy, sad, angry, fearful, surprised, disgusted—from diverse individuals. Pay close attention to their facial expressions, body language, and vocal tone. For each clip, write down your observations. What microexpressions do you detect?
How do their postures and gestures reinforce or contradict their words? Compare your observations with descriptions of those emotions found within

the book. This exercise helps you to connect theoretical knowledge with real-world examples, improving your accuracy in identifying emotions from nonverbal cues. Repeat this exercise regularly, gradually increasing the complexity of the video clips you select, including those where emotions are more ambiguous or masked.

Next, focus on honing your ability to observe microexpressions. Start with still images depicting a range of emotions. Focus intently on the subtle changes in the face—the fleeting contractions of muscles around the eyes, mouth, and eyebrows—that reveal a person's true emotional state. Try to identify the specific microexpressions present. Then, search for videos showcasing interviews, debates or
everyday conversations. Challenge yourself to identify microexpressions in real-time, noting the context and the words spoken. This practice will help you to distinguish genuine emotion from feigned expressions, a critical skill in navigating complex social interactions. Consider recording yourself observing these videos, and reviewing your
analysis. This self-assessment allows for valuable self-reflection and identifies areas where you need to enhance your skills.

Beyond facial expressions, we must consider the importance of body language. For this exercise, find a public space where you can observe people without being intrusive (a coffee shop, park, or airport are good choices). Select a few individuals, and, without making eye contact, observe their body language. Note their posture, gestures, and overall demeanor. Try to infer their emotional state and what they might be thinking or feeling. Afterward, reflect on your observations. Did their body language align with the context of the situation? Did you notice any inconsistencies? This exercise helps you to contextualize nonverbal cues, improving your accuracy and reducing the likelihood of misinterpretations. Remember that context is critical. A slumped posture might indicate tiredness, sadness, or simply a comfortable resting position. Consider repeating this exercise in different settings to improve your ability to adjust your analysis to the situation.

Now let's move on to more complex scenarios. Find video clips or recordings of conversations or negotiations. These might include political debates, business meetings, or even casual conversations between friends. Analyze the interaction, paying close attention to both verbal and nonverbal communication. Consider the following: How does each person's body language support or contradict their words? Are there any microexpressions that reveal underlying emotions or intentions? How does the overall dynamic of the interaction shift based on nonverbal cues?

Document your observations, providing a detailed explanation of your analysis and your conclusions. This exercise develops your ability to interpret complex interactions, where multiple nonverbal cues are operating simultaneously. The focus should be on identifying patterns, and understanding how different nonverbal cues interact to paint a clearer, more nuanced picture of the situation.

The next challenge focuses on active listening and mirroring.

Find a partner (a friend, family member, or colleague) and engage in a conversation about a topic you both find engaging. Focus on actively listening to your partner, observing their body language as they speak. Subtly mirror their postures and gestures. This builds rapport and improves your ability to pick up on subtle shifts in mood. Then, switch roles, observe your partner mirroring you, and compare your experiences. Discuss the way your nonverbal behaviors influenced the flow of the conversation. This exercise fosters empathy and a stronger understanding of how nonverbal mirroring can affect relationships and communication.

To further enhance your understanding, consider participating in structured observation exercises available online or through workshops. These opportunities provide a controlled environment where you can practice your skills with feedback from trained professionals. Additionally, explore the extensive body of research and resources available on nonverbal communication and microexpressions. This ongoing learning will enrich your understanding and refine your observational abilities.

One of the most powerful aspects of mastering the art of reading people is enhancing your own self-awareness. Begin paying closer attention to your own nonverbal cues. Record yourself during conversations, presentations or even solo thoughts. Analyze your own body language: What are your habitual postures? How do your facial expressions change throughout the course of a conversation? Understanding your own nonverbal communication will help you recognize similar cues in others and refine your interpretations.

Finally, remember that the ethical application of these skills is paramount. Use your newfound abilities to foster stronger connections, improve communication, and navigate social situations with greater empathy and understanding. Avoid making judgments or assumptions based on limited
information. Instead, seek to understand the context and motivations behind the nonverbal cues you observe.

These exercises are designed to be a starting point. As your skills develop, you can adapt and modify them to suit your own learning style and goals. The continuous practice and refinement of your observation skills, combined with a strong understanding of the underlying principles of nonverbal communication, will enable you to navigate the complexities of human interaction with confidence and insight. The journey toward mastery is ongoing. Embrace the challenge and let this knowledge enrich your life. The world is full of untold stories, and the ability to read between the lines – to see beyond words – unlocks a depth of understanding that transcends the surface. The more you practice, the more proficient you will become, and the more rewarding your ability to understand the unspoken will become. This skill serves as a powerful tool for building stronger relationships, navigating complex situations, and enhancing your overall effectiveness in personal and professional life. So continue to practice, continue to learn, and continue to refine your skillset. The rewards are far-reaching and deeply rewarding.

AUTHOR BIOGRAPHY

Meet Sam Tiwana, a Renaissance entrepreneur whose expertise spans from closing multimillion-dollar deals to spotting rare birds and getting lost in the improvisational flow of jazz. With one foot in real estate and the other in the digital world, he's all about smart risks, bold moves, and pivoting faster than his Tesla on autopilot (which he, of course, loves).

Sam's approach to life isn't just about getting ahead; it's about savoring the ride. Inspired by the Japanese philosophy of "kaizen"—fancy for "small steps to big change"—he's always leveling up in ways that look effortless. He has a knack for spotting the patterns that others miss, whether it's in the market, the jazz tune playing, or out in nature on a bird-watching break.

At home, Sam's got three tech-savvy kids deeply invested in crypto, programming, and real estate themselves. He's raised them with the perfect mix of future-forward thinking and old-school values, keeping the Tiwana family both grounded and ready to adapt to whatever the digital landscape throws next.

Through his writing, Sam weaves together business acumen, life wisdom, and refreshing humor, offering readers a unique roadmap to success that's as practical as it is inspiring.